Sports Illustrated

ANY GIVEN NUMBER

THE ULTIMATE SPORTS DEBATE
Who Wore It Best, from 00 to 99

CONTENTS

They wore some of the most famous numbers in sports, but one digit mattered most to the Reds in the 1976 World Series: Four, as in how many games it took them to sweep the Yankees.

Stephen Cannella *Editor* | **Steven Hoffman** *Creative Director* | **Bill Syken** *Writer*

Cristina Scalet *Photo Editor* | **Kevin Kerr** *Copy Editor* | **Josh Denkin** *Designer*

Stephanie Apstein *Reporter* | **Porter Binks** *Photo Researcher* | **Stefanie Kaufman** *Project Manager*

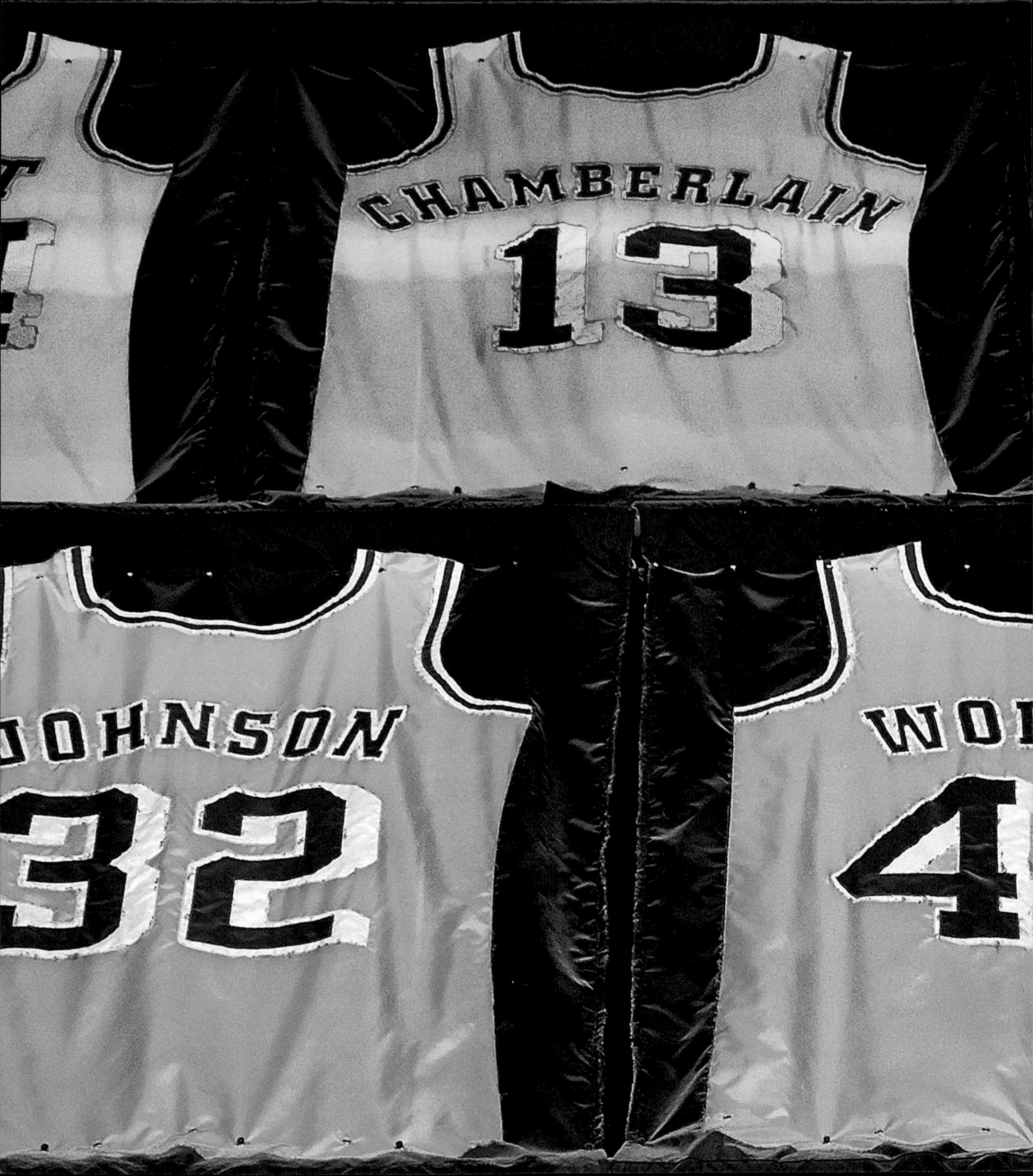
CHAMBERLAIN
13
JOHNSON
32

Not afterthoughts, rafterthoughts: The Lakers' retired jerseys hang high in the Staples Center.

The pillars of the Oilers' 1980s dynasty are honored with banners at Edmonton's Rexall Place.

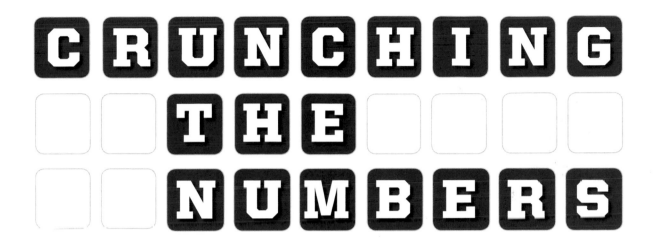

CRUNCHING THE NUMBERS

Perfect numbers, like perfect men, are very rare.
—RENÉ DESCARTES

THE WORLD TOOK LITTLE NOTICE SOME 35 YEARS AGO WHEN A BOY in Wilmington, North Carolina, chose 23 as his high school uniform number. Michael Jordan's older brother Larry wore 45, so Michael did the math, halving it and dutifully rounding off to the higher number, an occasion that marked, quite possibly, the last time the future King of Air thought of himself as a half of anything. And by the time Michael turned himself into gold-plated legend, the number 23 had become—at least in a sports context, Monsieur Descartes—close to perfect.

Since there are no objective standards for linking athlete and jersey number, we have no illusions that you will find our choices perfect in *Any Given Number*. (Though we would like to see the argument for assigning anyone else besides Jordan number 23, especially since LeBron James gave it up years ago and went to 6.) This number thing is intense and personal with a hint of the mystical. If you grew up wearing a Bill Walton–

style headband, rooting for UCLA and listening to the Grateful Dead, well, then no argument for Jim Brown, Magic Johnson, Sandy Koufax, Steve Carlton, O.J. Simpson or Karl Malone will convince you that 32 does not belong for all eternity to the Big Redhead.

Some athletes, after all, are destined from the womb to wear a certain jersey number. Penguins superstar Sidney Crosby came into the world on 8/7/87, born to his future number 87. Fans on the South Side of Chicago knew on what spring day to serenade a White Sox leftfielder in the 1970s, since Carlos May, who wore 17 right under his name, was born on 5/17 in the year of 1948. Alas, former NFL player Dean May was not given the chance to be May 26 since, as a quarterback, he was mandated to wear a number below 20 for the two seasons he spent in the league.

A minor league player from the 1950s had a more unusual approach to his name and birthdate. John Neves wore a backward number 7, "Seven" being the backward spelling of "Neves." We assume that Ɣ did not also find it necessary to distinguish himself from a slightly more celebrated number 7; Neves hit .240 in his one season (1951) with the Fargo-Moorhead Twins of the Northern League, while Mickey Mantle hit 536 home runs on bad knees.

A PLAYER'S CONNECTION WITH NUMBERS CAN go deeper than birthdays, as is the case with veteran winger Jaromir Jagr, who has worn his 68 with all seven of his NHL teams. Jagr's choice was based not

only upon the year (1968) of the "Prague Spring," when Czechoslovakians tried to liberalize their country only to be squashed by a Soviet invasion, but also the year that his grandfather died.

Less political reasoning gave Kevyn Adams number 42 when he signed with the Maple Leafs—the center was a fan of *The Hitchhiker's Guide to the Galaxy*, in which 42 was presented as the answer to, well, just about everything. In Major League Baseball today, it's the answer to only one thing—Jackie Robinson's universally retired number, especially since Mariano Rivera, the best allowed 42, has departed the pen.

Indeed, jersey numbers are important to the preservation of league history and especially franchise history, the number-retirement ceremony often taking

Some athletes are destined from the womb to wear a certain jersey. But the connection to a number can go deeper than a birthday.

on the atmosphere of sacred ritual, particularly in history-heavy cities like Boston (21 retired Celtics numbers) and New York (15 retired by the Yankees). And who can forget the moving moment when the Marlins retired 5 for the late Carl Barger? Actually, just about everyone. Barger, the first president of the franchise, never played and chose the number in honor of his

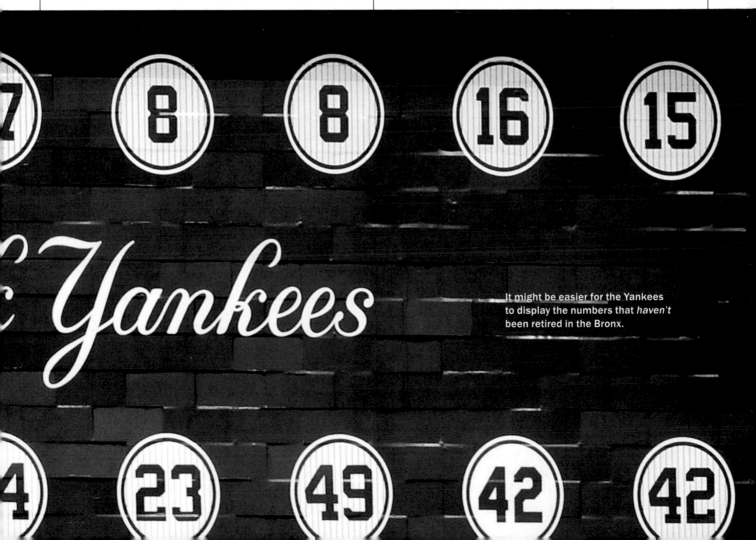

It might be easier for the Yankees to display the numbers that *haven't* been retired in the Bronx.

> *Sports convey upon numbers a certain distinction they wouldn't otherwise have except, perhaps, at high-level math conferences.*

favorite player, Joe DiMaggio, also our favorite *cinco*.

Actually, 5 is back in circulation in Miami, something that happens from time to time. As seriously as we might take those digits on the back of a jersey, players do change them. When Prince Fielder was traded from Detroit to Texas, he switched from 28 to 84, both because he was born in 1984 and because he wanted something "fresh." Those are common reasons. Even superstar athletes closely associated with a specific number make alterations from time to time, as when Kobe Bryant tripled from 8 to 24, a return, he said, to his high school number. And it's worth remembering that Jordan went with 45 (or 2 x 22.5) for a while when he returned to the NBA because the Bulls had wasted no time retiring 23 after His Airness left the game for a season and a half to play baseball.

On occasion, there's not much sentimentality attached to numbers. Braves owner Ted Turner once ordered that Andy Messersmith sport the word CHANNEL on his back, directly over his number 17—making the pitcher a walking billboard for the television station that showed Braves games. (The commissioner's office quickly nixed the idea.) So even as Messersmith became one of the early icons of free agency in the mid-70s, he was also a symbol for ownership crassness.

On occasion, jersey numbers have engendered disharmony among teammates. But number disputes are generally settled amicably, because the player who is asked to give up the number has little to gain by keeping it (he isn't famous) and much to gain by surrendering it (the famous guy will pay). Former Braves outfielder Brian Jordan once bought a $40,000 motorcycle for Harley-loving third base coach Fredi Gonzalez in exchange for number 33, a fact that also raises the question: What's a third base coach doing with a prime number like 33? Fredi is back wearing it now, but at least he's calling the shots as Atlanta's manager.

Carlos Delgado went for bling when he gave 21 to Toronto teammate Roger Clemens before the 1997 season, picking up a Rolex from the Rocket. In a complicated bit of homage-numerology, Clemens couldn't get 21 when he went to Houston seven years later because teammate Andy Pettitte had requested it in tribute to Clemens. All this occurred, of course, before both of their numbers came up in a banned-substance scandal.

Utilityman Joe McEwing chose a more domestic prize, earning financing for a home baby nursery from Tom Glavine in exchange for giving up his 47 when the pitcher joined the Mets before the 2003 season.

Chris Kluwe, the former Vikings punter, had a shopping list of conditions before he would surrender jersey 5 to Donovan McNabb in 2011. The quarterback had to give $5,000 to the charity of Kluwe's choice; he had to mention Kluwe's band (Tripping Icarus) five times in a press conference; and he had to buy the punter an ice cream cone. We don't have a Kluwe as to whether all those conditions were met, but it doesn't much matter now—both left Minnesota under unhappy circumstances.

HE PRIZE FOR NUMBER bartering probably goes to another punter, Jeff Feagles, who kicked for five teams over a 22-year career that ended in 2009. He first sold his number 10 to Eli Manning for a week's vacation in Florida, then got an outdoor kitchen for his home in Phoenix for surrendering 17 to Plaxico Burress. (Question: Isn't all of Phoenix an outdoor kitchen?)

As important as jersey numbers have become, they weren't always around as player-identifiers. When Babe Ruth socked his 60th home run in 1927, his jersey was bereft of the now iconic 3, which the Yankees added in 1929, assigning the digits based on a player's spot in the batting order. (Ruth famously hit third, number 4 Lou Gehrig was the cleanup guy, number 5 Bob Meusel hit fifth etc.) And football, believe it or not, did not always have the regimented jersey-number system it has now; in one gloriously incongruous example, quarterback Otto Graham used to scamper around in number 60 before being forced into a QB number (14) in 1952, the

The cold and the bold: Lambeau Field is ringed with the numbers of Packers greats.

RETIRED NUMBERS

14	3	15	66	92
DON HUTSON	TONY CANADEO	BART STARR	RAY NITSCHKE	REGGIE WHIT

seventh year of his Hall of Fame career. The Browns have retired Otto's 14 but 60 remains available. (And speaking of retired Ottos, no one will again wear the 00 worn by Raiders center Jim—the NFL has since nullified the use of null-numbered jerseys.)

The NFL-mandated number system was put in place primarily so that referees could identity ineligible receivers downfield. Now it exists primarily so referees can out otherwise anonymous offensive linemen for holding. But that's one of the few negatives attached to sports numbers, which, by and large, have organically connected to athletes in a positive way.

Similarly, sports conveys upon numbers a certain distinction they wouldn't otherwise have except, perhaps, at high-level mathematics conferences. Is there anyone besides the occasional fertility specialist who thinks first of chromosomes, not MJ, when the number 23 comes up in conversation?

Yes, though we yearn in our real lives not to be considered "just a number," when we put on a jersey and walk onto the playing field sometimes that's sometimes all we are . . . and we're O.K. with that. □

00

THE DEBATE

THIS BOOK will revel in the task of comparing apples to oranges. So it is fitting that we begin by assessing the relative merits of **Jim Otto** and **Robert Parish**—two centers whose similarities begin and end with the name of the positions they played.

Otto was indisputably the best center in the history of the AFL: The longtime Raider was an all-league selection in each of the 10 years of the AFL's existence. He also made two All-NFL teams after the leagues' 1970 merger, and he was inducted into the Pro Football Hall of Fame in 1980. But spending the prime of his career in the AFL, where he faced a lower level of competition than he would have in the NFL, is a mark against Otto.

Parish, meanwhile, stood tall against some of the all-time greats in his sport. The seven-footer teamed with Larry Bird and Kevin McHale in the iconic frontcourt that led the Celtics to three NBA titles in the 1980s. Parish earned those rings by taking on three of the league's legendary big men in the NBA Finals: Moses Malone in '81, Kareem Abdul-Jabbar in '84 and Hakeem Olajuwon in '86.

In a way the stoic Parish was the perfect 00: neither positive nor negative, the number matched his usually expressionless demeanor. If he is ever to be usurped as the greatest 0/00 (we considered both versions of zero together) the candidate will likely come from the NBA, where the number is more popular than ever; today there's a 0 on about half the league's rosters. Thunder guard **Russell Westbrook** leads a pack of up-and-comers that includes Trail Blazers guard and 2012–13 Rookie of the Year **Damian Lillard**. But for now, Parish is the hero among zeroes.

→ THE VERDICT
ROBERT PARISH

ALL FOR NAUGHT

The NFL banned the use of 0/00 in 1973, but not before writer GEORGE PLIMPTON wore it when he played for Detroit in the preseason for his 1966 book *Paper Lion*. . . . In baseball several players of note wore 0/00 for a season late in their careers, including DON BAYLOR (A's), BOBBY BONDS (Cardinals), JOSE CANSECO (Blue Jays), JACK CLARK (Padres) and OSCAR GAMBLE (White Sox).

CONTENDERS

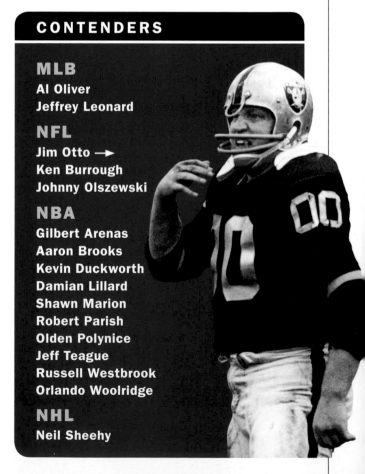

MLB
Al Oliver
Jeffrey Leonard

NFL
Jim Otto →
Ken Burrough
Johnny Olszewski

NBA
Gilbert Arenas
Aaron Brooks
Kevin Duckworth
Damian Lillard
Shawn Marion
Robert Parish
Olden Polynice
Jeff Teague
Russell Westbrook
Orlando Woolridge

NHL
Neil Sheehy

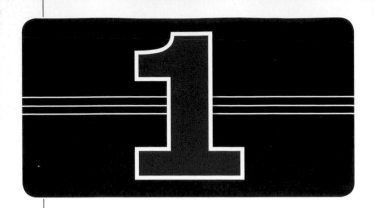

1

THE DEBATE

SOME ATHLETES don't need a foam finger to declare themselves number 1—they can just point to their jersey. Interestingly, while multiple 1s have made it to the Halls of Fame in baseball, football and hockey, not a single player in the NBA—whose athletes are not collectively known for their modesty—who wore the number has been enshrined. It's possible **Chauncey Billups** and/or **Tracy McGrady** will put an end to that, but even so the discussion centers on three non-hoops candidates: **Ozzie Smith** in baseball, **Jacques Plante** and **Warren Moon** in hockey and in football.

The nod goes to Smith, the best defensive player in the history of the game. The Wizard owned the web gem before the term existed, but beyond his lengthy highlight reel the longtime Cardinal was remarkably consistent, setting records for assists and double plays by a shortstop. He also accumulated 2,460 hits in 19 seasons.

Smith is given a hard run by Plante, who won seven Vezina Trophies, led the Canadiens to five straight Stanley Cups from 1956 to '60 and literally changed the face of hockey by becoming the first goaltender to wear a mask regularly. Moon was a trailblazer of a different kind, as one of the few African-American quarterbacks of his era. After going undrafted out of college in 1978 he won five straight CFL championships before NFL decision-makers believed in his ability. He had nine 3,000-yard passing seasons for the Oilers, Vikings and Seahawks at a time when such totals were rare. But neither Plante nor Moon, unlike Smith, can unequivocally be called the best in any aspect of his sport—which is why Ozzie is No. 1 among numbers 1.

➤ THE VERDICT
OZZIE SMITH

AMONG THE CHOSEN ONES

Upon his arrival in Orlando, ANFERNEE HARDAWAY wanted to wear 25, his college number at Memphis State. But it was taken by guard NICK ANDERSON, so Hardaway chose 1—a much better fit for someone whose nickname was Penny. . . . Besides WARREN MOON, the seven NFL Hall of Famers to wear 1 all played in the leather-helmet years. The most notable: Packers icon CURLY LAMBEAU.

CONTENDERS

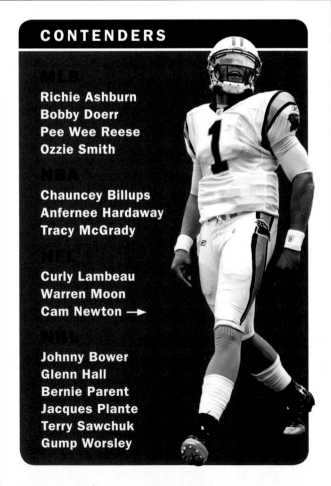

MLB

Richie Ashburn
Bobby Doerr
Pee Wee Reese
Ozzie Smith

NBA

Chauncey Billups
Anfernee Hardaway
Tracy McGrady

NFL

Curly Lambeau
Warren Moon
Cam Newton ➤

NHL

Johnny Bower
Glenn Hall
Bernie Parent
Jacques Plante
Terry Sawchuk
Gump Worsley

THE DEBATE

IN AN ATHLETIC contest between a man and a horse, the first instinct is to bet on the horse—especially if the horse is the legendary **Secretariat**. But what if the man is **Derek Jeter?**

Secretariat is the greatest racehorse ever, and while thoroughbreds aren't consistently identified with the same number the way that athletes are, he had a 2 on his side when he ran his greatest race: the 1973 Belmont, when he romped to the Triple Crown in a 31-length runaway, still a record for margin of victory.

Problem is, Secretariat didn't wear number 2 for his other Triple Crown wins. The real issue isn't horse versus man, it's a day versus a career—and Jeter's advantage here makes that Belmont win look like a nail-biter. The shortstop is the Yankees' alltime hit leader, the calm and charismatic captain who led his team to five World Series championships. And yet, impressive as they are, numbers don't begin to measure his baseball instincts, his charisma or his grace on his sport's biggest stages.

The third contender here is **Moses Malone**, a rebounding machine whose candidacy suffers from a variation of Secretariat's shortcoming: He achieved glorious heights wearing number 2, but didn't wear it all the time. Malone won three NBA MVP awards, but only one as a 2. That was the 1982–83 season, when he led the 76ers on their historic "fo' fo' fo'" rip through the postseason. But Malone had previously worn 24 while winning two MVP awards with the Rockets, only switching to 2 when he came to Philadelphia and found his number taken by sixth-man Bobby Jones. Had Malone worn number 2 his entire career he might give Jeter a run. But the shortstop glides to the finish line.

→ THE VERDICT

DEREK JETER

TWO OF A KIND

Rockies shortstop TROY TULOWITZKI, a three-time All-Star, wears number 2 as a tribute to Jeter, a 13-time All-Star. . . . When he joined the Falcons in 2008, quarterback MATT RYAN couldn't have number 12, which he wore at Boston College, because it was taken by receiver Michael Jenkins, so Ryan switched to 2. His first NFL pass was a 62-yard touchdown to Jenkins.

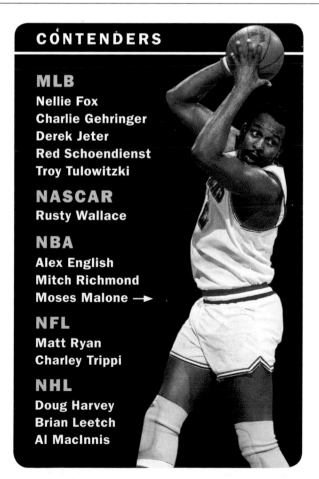

CONTENDERS

MLB
Nellie Fox
Charlie Gehringer
Derek Jeter
Red Schoendienst
Troy Tulowitzki

NASCAR
Rusty Wallace

NBA
Alex English
Mitch Richmond
Moses Malone →

NFL
Matt Ryan
Charley Trippi

NHL
Doug Harvey
Brian Leetch
Al MacInnis

19

3

GOOD THINGS COME IN THREES

In 3½ seasons with the Yankees light-hitting outfielder CLIFF MAPES managed to wear No. 3 before it was retired for BABE RUTH in 1948, and No. 7 before it was ever donned by Mickey Mantle. . . . If there's an NBA equivalent of Ruth and DALE EARNHARDT for rising from hardscrabble beginnings to wild popularity and success, it's point guard ALLEN IVERSON, who grew up dirt-poor, was imprisoned in high school and in his prime had the NBA's top-selling jersey.

CONTENDERS

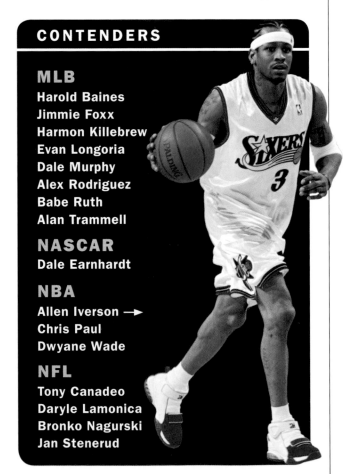

MLB
Harold Baines
Jimmie Foxx
Harmon Killebrew
Evan Longoria
Dale Murphy
Alex Rodriguez
Babe Ruth
Alan Trammell

NASCAR
Dale Earnhardt

NBA
Allen Iverson →
Chris Paul
Dwyane Wade

NFL
Tony Canadeo
Daryle Lamonica
Bronko Nagurski
Jan Stenerud

THERE REALLY IS no debate here, but for fun let's test-drive a contrarian argument just to see how it feels: **Dale Earnhardt** is the best athlete associated with the number 3.

Earnhardt (*below*) was already a mythic NASCAR figure before he died at age 49 in a crash on the final lap of the 2001 Daytona 500. Not only had he equaled Richard Petty's mark of seven season championships, he had done so with an aggressive driving style that fans adored. Even though The Intimidator was a superstar, he maintained the aura of a blue-collar guy in the bluest-collar sport. His death only enhanced his legend and further elevated his status as a racing icon.

Earnhardt is so accomplished and so beloved, in fact, that it's tempting to say he is the **Babe Ruth** of auto racing—and that's where the argument that anyone but Ruth should own number 3 begins to fall apart. Because the Babe was more than a baseball star and the most popular athlete of his era. He was a cultural icon, a one-man metaphor for excellence in any field. If you're the Babe Ruth of podiatrists, suddenly podiatry sounds like a pretty cool line of work to be in.

Want stats? Ruth is the game's greatest slugger—but he also has the 17th-best ERA in history. (Yes, he pitched too.) And with all due respect to Earnhardt, no athlete ever connected with the fan better than the Babe. He created the archetype of the modern slugger, and his exploits on and off the field made him the perfect Jazz Age superstar. A full century after his career began, he is still the Babe Ruth of sports.

Before shutting down the discussion, a kind word for two NFL 3s: legendary running back **Bronko Nagurski** and **Jan Stenerud**, the only pure placekicker in the Pro Football Hall of Fame. At any other number they would deserve more attention. But regardless of number, everyone else is eclipsed by the Babe.

→ **THE VERDICT**

BABE RUTH

4

THE DEBATE

THREE ATHLETES who wore number 4 are sports demigods, legends who would come out on top in virtually any comparison. But they can't all be the best here.

It has to be **Brett Favre**, right? The quarterback rewrote the record book (with career marks for completions, passing yardage and touchdown passes) at the most important position in the most popular game in America, and he did it with gunslinging flair. Yes, his impetuousness on the field and indecision off it frustrated Green Bay fans and led to his ugly exit from the Packers. But his talent and toughness (321 consecutive starts) far outweighed those flaws.

Speaking of consecutive starts, the choice at number 4 has to be **Lou Gehrig**, right? The greatest first baseman ever played in 2,130 straight games and had the third-best slugging percentage ever. How respected was he? In 1927, when his Yankees teammate Babe Ruth hit 60 home runs, it was Gehrig who was named MVP. The Iron Horse was also the first major leaguer to have his number retired, and his "luckiest man" speech is one of the iconic moments in sports.

Speaking of iconic moments, **Bobby Orr** is the choice at number 4, for far more than the Stanley Cup-winning goal he scored for the Bruins in 1970. (Though the image of Orr, arms raised in celebration as he literally flies across the crease, is legendary.) Orr, quite simply, transformed hockey. Before him, defensemen were just that: defenders. Orr led the NHL in scoring in 1969–70, and at the same time was rugged in his own zone. Orr scored 100 points in a season six times, before his knees failed him too young. He was forced to retire at 30—but he left behind a sport changed forever.

➤ THE VERDICT
BOBBY ORR

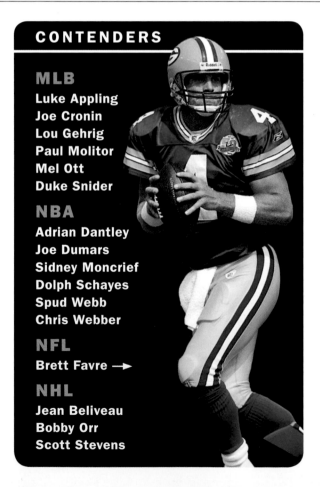

CONTENDERS

MLB
Luke Appling
Joe Cronin
Lou Gehrig
Paul Molitor
Mel Ott
Duke Snider

NBA
Adrian Dantley
Joe Dumars
Sidney Moncrief
Dolph Schayes
Spud Webb
Chris Webber

NFL
Brett Favre ➤

NHL
Jean Beliveau
Bobby Orr
Scott Stevens

5

THE DEBATE

WITH ALL DUE respect to other sports, the number 5 belongs to baseball. Consider that **Brooks Robinson** and **George Brett**, two of the best third basemen ever, can't even crack the top three ballplayers at this number. Nor does Hall of Fame slugger **Hank Greenberg**, who led the American League in home runs four times in the 1930s and '40s.

No, the top-three countdown begins with **Albert Pujols**, the best offensive player of his era. Before joining the Angels in 2012 he won three NL MVP awards for the Cardinals and is the only player in history to hit .300 with at least 30 home runs and 100 RBIs in each of his first 10 seasons. He has two Gold Gloves and two World Series wins for good measure.

Ahead of Pujols there is **Johnny Bench**, as complete a catcher as the game has seen. A two-time MVP, he was the anchor of Cincinnati's 1970s Big Red Machine, twice led the NL in home runs, and may have been the best defensive catcher ever.

But there is great, and then there is **Joe DiMaggio**. The Yankee Clipper has the numbers and the accolades: three MVPs, .325 career average, nine World Series rings. But he also captured the American imagination—for his grace in the field, for his 56-game hitting streak in 1941, even for his rocky marriage to Marilyn Monroe. "He had fame that transcended mere celebrity," Ron Fimrite wrote in SI in '99. "For nearly half a century after his playing days had ended, Joe DiMaggio remained a regal presence in the public eye, a species of American aristocrat. I've known people who couldn't tell an infield fly from a household pest who nevertheless held the Yankee Clipper in awe."

➤ THE VERDICT

JOE DIMAGGIO

DEPRIVED OF FIVE

When he came to the NFL in 2006, REGGIE BUSH wanted to wear 5, which had been his number in high school and at USC—but NFL rules said running backs must wear numbers 20-49. He switched to 25, buying the number from Saints teammate Fred McAfee for a charitable donation. . . . Two members of Michigan's Fab Five, JUWAN HOWARD and JALEN ROSE, wore the number 5 in the NBA.

CONTENDERS

MLB
Jeff Bagwell
Johnny Bench
George Brett
Joe DiMaggio
Hank Greenberg
Albert Pujols ➤
Brooks Robinson

NASCAR
Terry Labonte

NBA
Jason Kidd

NFL
Paul Hornung
Donovan McNabb

NHL
Bernie Geoffrion
Nicklas Lidstrom
Denis Potvin

6

THE DEBATE

THE BATTLE for number 6 is another fierce one. **Stan Musial** ambles into the discussion with his seven NL batting titles, three MVPs and status as the embodiment of the hometown hero. The Cardinals legend, a career .331 hitter, had 3,630 hits: 1,815 at home, 1,815 on the road. Even his trivia is cool.

Stan the Man is a distant contender, though, because he shares a number with **Bill Russell**, the best player on the greatest dynasty in professional sports. The Celtics' big man averaged 22.5 rebounds in his career; between his mastery of the glass and his shot-blocking skills, few players have been more intimidating in the paint. But the big stat is that Boston won 11 NBA titles in 13 seasons from 1956–57 to '68–69 with Russell in the lineup. Few players in any sport can match Russell's leadership and championship résumé.

Celtics architect Red Auerbach once told SI's George Plimpton this story about Russell's dominance of Neil Johnston, a talented scorer for the 1950s Philadelphia Warriors: "Russell destroyed him. He destroyed him psychologically as well, so that he practically ran him out of organized basketball. He blocked so many shots that Johnston began throwing his hook farther and farther from the basket. It was ludicrous, and the guys along the bench began to laugh, maybe in relief that they didn't have to worry about such a guy themselves."

If there's a wild card in this debate, it is **LeBron James**. He wore 23 for his first seven NBA seasons, but switched to 6 when he took his talents from Cleveland to Miami. While wearing 6 James matured from a stats-and-highlights guy to a winner—he has two titles and counting. But that's not enough to unseat Russell. Yet.

➤ THE VERDICT
BILL RUSSELL

SMALL IMPACT, HUGE HONOR

Two NBA teams, the Kings and the Magic, have retired the number 6 in honor of their fans, aka the Sixth Man. . . . Six major league franchises have retired 6, though the Padres did so somewhat dubiously. They honored STEVE GARVEY, who spent just five seasons in San Diego at the end of his career. He was the 1984 NLCS MVP with the Padres, but played 14 seasons for the Dodgers—who haven't retired his number.

CONTENDERS

MLB
Carl Furillo
Steve Garvey
Al Kaline
Stan Musial
Tony Oliva
Willie Wilson

NASCAR
Mark Martin

NBA
Walter Davis
Julius Erving
LeBron James ➔
Bill Russell

NFL
Rolf Benirschke

NHL
Ace Bailey
Phil Housley

7

PLAY THE NAME GAME

He doesn't get the nod here, but MICKEY MANTLE landed a greater honor: pop culture immortality, courtesy of *Seinfeld*. In one episode George tells his fiancée that if they have a child, he wants to name the baby Seven in honor of the Mick—then becomes enraged when another couple steals the name. Does a number as a baby name sound absurd? Not to soccer star DAVID BECKHAM and his wife Victoria: In 2011 they named their daughter Harper Seven Beckham.

CONTENDERS

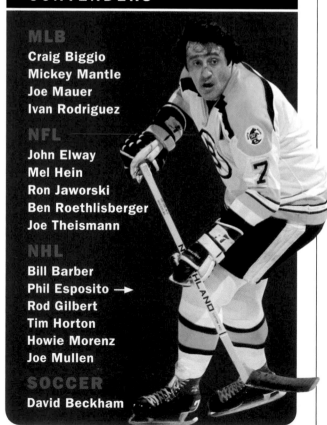

MLB
Craig Biggio
Mickey Mantle
Joe Mauer
Ivan Rodriguez

NFL
John Elway
Mel Hein
Ron Jaworski
Ben Roethlisberger
Joe Theismann

NHL
Bill Barber
Phil Esposito →
Rod Gilbert
Tim Horton
Howie Morenz
Joe Mullen

SOCCER
David Beckham

FOR FANS of a certain age, listening to the debate that follows may be like listening to someone make the case that Nirvana is more significant to the history of rock 'n' roll than Elvis Presley. But, blasphemous or not, we will make the argument: It's **John Elway** over **Mickey Mantle** at number 7.

The Mantle folktale is based largely on the towering home runs that were his signature. The legend took root in a 1951 Yankees exhibition game against USC, where a young Mantle *(below)* hit a ball so far out of Bovard Field—estimates had the shot traveling at least 550 feet—that it landed in the mid-

dle of a Trojans football practice. The term "tape-measure" shot was made for Mantle, because fans wanted to quantify what they saw. The switch-hitter delivered shots of at least 450 feet to the right- and leftfields of every AL stadium. This is how a legend spreads far and wide. That, and three MVP awards, a Triple Crown in 1956, and seven World Series titles in a 12-year span.

Elway, too, had a knack for amazing feats. His trademark was the fourth-quarter comeback and his most famous was "The Drive" in the 1986 AFC title game, when he marched his Broncos 98 yards in Cleveland to force overtime. In the course of his 16-year career Elway matured from rawly talented escape artist to field general. And while his two Super Bowl wins came with great supporting casts, he provided the signature moment of those wins. In Super Bowl XXXII, chasing his first ring, the 37-year-old Elway faced third-and-six in the third quarter with the Broncos and Packers tied. Elway scrambled toward a first down, and as he neared the marker he leaped and absorbed a hit from Green Bay's LeRoy Butler that spun Elway fully around in midair. When he landed he had picked up the first down. The Broncos scored to go ahead, and soon Elway finally had his ring. A year later he had another, and when he retired after that Super Bowl he had locked up the title of the greatest number 7.

➤ THE VERDICT

JOHN ELWAY

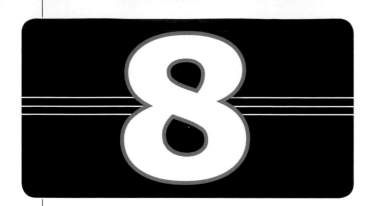

8

THE DEBATE

IF YOU'RE FUNNY, people don't take you seriously. **Yogi Berra** never said that, but it sounds like something he might have—and it aptly sums up the Hall of Fame catcher's legacy. Berra is so well-known for his Yogi-isms and wise-clown persona that it's easy to forget how great a player he was.

But we remember, and that's why Berra is the choice here despite some stiff competition: Super Bowl–winning quarterbacks **Troy Aikman** and **Steve Young**, and baseball legends **Carl Yastrzemski** and **Cal Ripken Jr**.

Ripken, a two-time MVP and 19-time All-Star at shortstop and third base, is also baseball's Iron Man: In 1995 he passed Lou Gehrig's record of 2,130 consecutive games played. Like Ripken, who finished his career with 3,184 hits, Yastrzemski is a member of the 3,000-hit club (he had 3,419), and after the Red Sox legend won the 1967 Triple Crown baseball wouldn't see another player claim one for 45 years.

Those résumés are impressive, but Berra's surpasses them all. The heart and soul of the Yankees dynasties of the '50s, he won three MVP awards and had a seven-year stretch during which he never finished lower than fourth in the voting. When Don Larsen threw his perfect game in the '56 World Series, who do you think was behind the plate? That game was an aberration for Larsen, who otherwise had a middling career, but it was right on track for Berra, who was on the receiving end of 173 shutouts. He was also a fixture in the Fall Classic: Berra won 10 World Series rings, the most of any player in baseball history. As he might say himself, Yogi won too much. That's why he can't lose here.

➤ THE VERDICT

YOGI BERRA

LATE TO EIGHT, BUT STILL GREAT

Another great baseball 8, JOE MORGAN, began his career as an 18. But when the Astros traded him to the Reds for Lee May and Tommy Helms in 1971—bad trade, by the way—he couldn't have 18 because it belonged to Ted Kluszewski, a former Reds star turned coach. So Morgan switched to 8, as a tribute to one of his favorite players, WILLIE STARGELL. Morgan, like Stargell, is enshrined in the Hall of Fame.

CONTENDERS

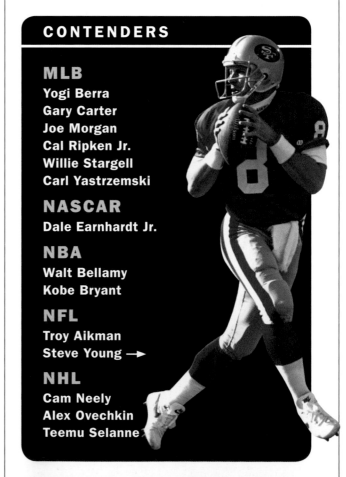

MLB
Yogi Berra
Gary Carter
Joe Morgan
Cal Ripken Jr.
Willie Stargell
Carl Yastrzemski

NASCAR
Dale Earnhardt Jr.

NBA
Walt Bellamy
Kobe Bryant

NFL
Troy Aikman
Steve Young ➤

NHL
Cam Neely
Alex Ovechkin
Teemu Selanne

9

HE CARRIED THAT WEIGHT

Canadiens right wing MAURICE (THE ROCKET) RICHARD, who set several records that Howe would break, also wore 9, but he actually began his career wearing 15. After struggling in that number during his rookie season of 1942–43—he played so poorly that Montreal nearly traded him to the Rangers—Richard switched from 15 to 9, choosing the number to honor the birth of his first child, nine-pound daughter Huguette.

CONTENDERS

MLB
Roger Maris
Bill Mazeroski
Ted Williams

NASCAR
Bill Elliott

NBA
Richie Guerin
Tony Parker
Bob Pettit

NFL
Drew Brees →
Sonny Jurgensen

NHL
John Bucyk
Gordie Howe
Bobby Hull
Mike Modano
Maurice Richard

THE DEBATE

IT'S TEMPTING to define 9 as the tough-old-bird number. The contestants are two of the hardest men to play their respective sports: Mr. Hockey vs. Teddy Ballgame. **Sonny Jurgensen** (with your five NFL passing titles) and **Bob Pettit** (with your career NBA averages of 26.4 points and 16.2 rebounds), you're worthy of your respective Halls of Fame, but you might want to stay out of the middle of this one.

When **Gordie Howe** *(below)* retired, he held the NHL records for goals and assists—they'd be broken by Wayne Gretzky—but beyond scoring, Howe was the epitome of on-ice toughness.

(Heck, he invented the Gordie Howe hat trick: a goal, an assist and a fight in the same game.) Even as he played into his 50s, he wasn't above roughing up opponents with his trademark elbows. In 1980, as her husband was playing his 32nd and final pro season, Colleen Howe told SI, "Gordie doesn't elbow somebody in the jaw out of anger; he does it to teach them a lesson, if they've embarrassed him on the ice. He's a tremendously prideful person."

Ted Williams could appreciate that kind of attitude. Williams set out to be the greatest hitter that ever lived, and it's hard to argue he wasn't. His career average: .344, tied for seventh-best alltime. His on-base percentage: .482, the best ever. His slugging percentage: .634, second-best. In 1941 he batted .406; no one has hit .400 since. He also smacked 521 home runs, a total depressed by the prime seasons he sacrificed to serve as a Marine pilot in World War II and the Korean War.

In his poem "If," Rudyard Kipling defines what it means to be a man: "If you can talk with crowds and keep your virtue/Or walk with Kings—nor lose the common touch . . . If you can fill the unforgiving minute/With sixty seconds' worth of distance run." It's as if Kipling were describing Williams, who, like Joe DiMaggio, defined not just baseball greatness, but a certain species of American hero.

THE VERDICT
TED WILLIAMS

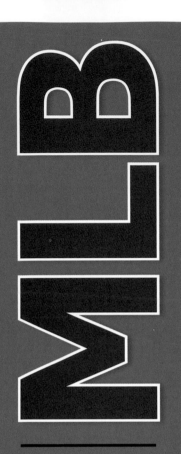

MLB

BY THE NUMBERS

What jersey has the richest history at each position? If you were to build a team by numbers, these are the digits you'd want to draft at each spot

FIRST BASE 5

Jeff Bagwell, Hank Greenberg, Albert Pujols
Next best: 3 (Jimmie Foxx, Harmon Killebrew, Bill Terry) and 25 (Jason Giambi, Mark McGwire, Rafael Palmeiro, Jim Thome)

SECOND BASE 2

Charlie Gehringer, Red Schoendienst
Next best: 15 (Davey Lopes, Dustin Pedroia), 12 (Roberto Alomar, Jeff Kent, Eddie Stanky) and 42 (Jackie Robinson)

THIRD BASE 5

George Brett, Brooks Robinson, David Wright
Next best: 10 (Ron Cey, Chipper Jones, Ron Santo) and 11 (Ken Caminiti, Darrell Evans, Toby Harrah, Ryan Zimmerman)

SHORTSTOP 1

Pee Wee Reese, Ozzie Smith, Garry Templeton
Next best: 2 (Derek Jeter, Hanley Ramirez, Troy Tulowitzki) and 11 (Luis Aparicio, Jim Fregosi, Barry Larkin, Jimmy Rollins)

CATCHER 8

Yogi Berra, Bob Boone, Gary Carter, Bill Dickey, Rick Ferrell, Ray Fosse, Javy Lopez
Next best: 7 (Joe Mauer, Ivan Rodriguez)

LEFTFIELD 8

Albert Belle, Willie Stargell, Carl Yastrzemski
Next best: 24 (Barry Bonds, Rickey Henderson, Manny Ramirez) and 9 (Minnie Minoso, Hank Sauer, Ted Williams)

CENTERFIELD 24

Ken Griffey Jr., Willie Mays, Jimmy Wynn
Next best: 7 (Kenny Lofton, Mickey Mantle) and 10 (Andre Dawson, Lloyd Waner, Vernon Wells)

RIGHTFIELD 44

Hank Aaron, Reggie Jackson
Next best: 21 (Roberto Clemente, Paul O'Neill, Sammy Sosa) and 3 (Harold Baines, Dale Murphy, Babe Ruth)

RIGHTHANDED PITCHER 45

Bob Gibson, Pedro Martinez, Steve Rogers
Next best: 35 (Mike Mussina, Phil Niekro, Justin Verlander, Bob Welch) and 22 (Roger Clemens, Jim Palmer, Mark Prior)

LEFTHANDED PITCHER 32

Steve Carlton, Sandy Koufax, Jon Matlack
Next best: 16 (Whitey Ford, Scott McGregor, Hal Newhouser, Frank Viola) and 47 (Tom Glavine, Gio Gonzalez, Bruce Hurst)

RELIEF PITCHER 42

Mariano Rivera, Bruce Sutter
Next best: 54 (Rich Gossage, Brad Lidge) and 49 (Armando Benitez, Rob Dibble, Jose Mesa, Hoyt Wilhelm)

Most Worn   **22**
846 players, 10 of them Hall of Famers

Least Worn   **80, 86, 89, 90, 92, 93**
They've never appeared on a big-league uni

Most MVPs   **5**
Eight players have combined for 14 trophies

Most World Series MVPs   **6**
Three each for Nos. 16, 20, 22, 23. 34, 45

Most Retired   **20**
Nine teams have hung it up

Reggie Jackson

10

THE DEBATE

THE NUMBER 10 belongs to soccer, as it has been worn by arguably the three greatest players in the history of the sport. **Lionel Messi** may be the world's best player right now, and perhaps ever. The Barcelona superstar has won the world player of the year award an unprecedented four times in a row. Among alltime greats Messi might even have the edge over another number 10, **Diego Maradona**. When FIFA named its best player of the 20th century, the hero of Argentina's 1986 World Cup victory was a cowinner.

The man with whom Maradona shared that honor also wore 10—and he is our top 10: **Pelé**. Soccer player of the century? Pelé was so much more. In 1999 he was named Athlete of the Century across all sports by the International Olympic Committee. (Take that, Babe Ruth.)

The Black Pearl earned that distinction by dominating South American soccer with a parade of spectacular goals—he had a record 1,281 in his career—and by leading Brazil to World Cup victories in 1958, '62 and '70. He was such a star that when he came out of retirement in '75 to play for the New York Cosmos of the upstart North American Soccer League, he instantly raised the profile of a sport that had been largely ignored by U.S. audiences.

The leader of the nonsoccer division of 10s would be **Guy Lafleur**, the Canadiens right wing who helped bring five Stanley Cups to Montreal; followed closely by longtime Braves slugger **Chipper Jones**, a model of excellence for two decades and a certain Hall of Famer. But good as they were, Lafleur and Jones can't even say they were the best in their sports. Pelé, on the other hand, is the perfect 10.

➤ THE VERDICT

PELÉ

WINNING WITH A PAIR OF 10S

After being traded to the Knicks in 1971, EARL MONROE formed the "Rolls-Royce backcourt" with WALT FRAZIER. There was one issue: Both players wore 10. As the new arrival, Monroe switched briefly to 33, and then later 15. Both ended up having their numbers retired by the team. . . . When he signed with the Nuggets in 2013, guard NATE ROBINSON took 10 in honor of Messi, his favorite soccer player.

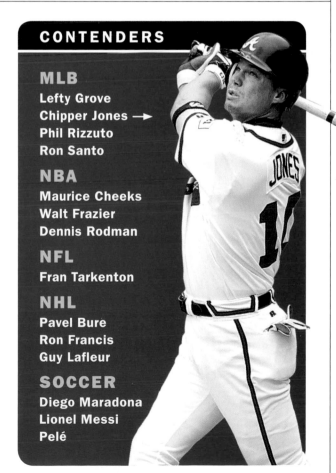

CONTENDERS

MLB
Lefty Grove
Chipper Jones ➤
Phil Rizzuto
Ron Santo

NBA
Maurice Cheeks
Walt Frazier
Dennis Rodman

NFL
Fran Tarkenton

NHL
Pavel Bure
Ron Francis
Guy Lafleur

SOCCER
Diego Maradona
Lionel Messi
Pelé

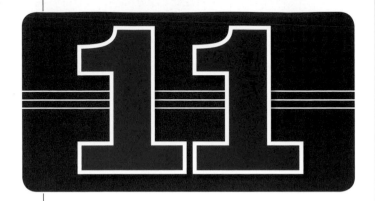

THE DEBATE

THE ATHLETES at number 11 make up what might be called Olympus's waiting room: They're Hall of Famers and alltime greats but most fall just short of true legendary status. Take **Isiah Thomas**: The point guard was the best player on the two-time champion Pistons and undoubtedly one of the best players of his generation—but he was overshadowed throughout his career by Michael Jordan. **Elvin Hayes** was an elite power forward and won an NBA title with the Bullets—but Kareem Abdul-Jabbar was unquestionably the best big man of his era. **Barry Larkin** was a Hall of Fame shortstop but didn't transcend the game like his contemporary Cal Ripken Jr. In football the top guys are **Norm Van Brocklin** and **Phil Simms**—both NFL champions, but each a clear step down from, say, Johnny Unitas or John Elway.

Of all the 11s, the one true legend is **Mark Messier**. He could do everything on the ice, from scoring to fighting to inspiring his teammates. Oh, could he inspire: The two-time NHL MVP was the quintessential captain, winning six Stanley Cups, including the one that ended the Rangers' 54-year title drought in 1994. And when those Rangers were facing elimination, down 2–1 in Game 6 of the Eastern Conference finals against New Jersey, Messier reeled off a series-saving hat trick.

Messier is second on the alltime lists for regular-season points and playoff points—trailing in both categories former Edmonton teammate Wayne Gretzky, without question the iconic NHL star of the 1980s and '90s. Still, Messier's leadership skills and championship pedigree place him a cut above the other near immortals at number 11.

➤ THE VERDICT

MARK MESSIER

FINALLY, THESE GO TO 11 . . .

When the NFL opened numbers 10–19 to wide receivers in 2004, the first three wideouts chosen in that year's draft, LARRY FITZGERALD, ROY WILLIAMS and REGGIE WILLIAMS, all took 11. . . . KARL MALONE wore 32 during his 18 years with the Jazz but switched to 11 for his final season, a one-year coda with the Lakers. Los Angeles had retired 32 for Magic Johnson.

CONTENDERS

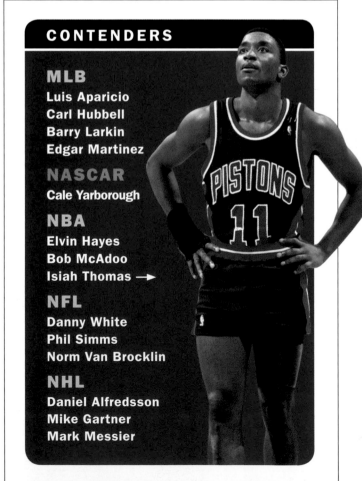

MLB
Luis Aparicio
Carl Hubbell
Barry Larkin
Edgar Martinez

NASCAR
Cale Yarborough

NBA
Elvin Hayes
Bob McAdoo
Isiah Thomas ➤

NFL
Danny White
Phil Simms
Norm Van Brocklin

NHL
Daniel Alfredsson
Mike Gartner
Mark Messier

THE DEBATE

THERE WAS A time when, if you were looking to win a Super Bowl, you pretty much had to have a quarterback with the number 12. It started with **Joe Namath**, who led the Jets to an upset of the Colts in Super Bowl III. **Roger Staubach** and the Cowboys won three years later, and then **Bob Griese** and the Dolphins took Super Bowls VII and VIII. The Steelers and **Terry Bradshaw** won four of the next six Super Bowls; the two that they missed went to Staubach and Co. and to the Raiders, quarterbacked by **Ken Stabler**.

The trend faded in the '80s and '90s, but in the 2000s **Tom Brady** again made 12 the number of NFL champions. Yes, the Patriots' QB has won one fewer Super Bowl than Bradshaw, but Brady is the pick because of how indisputably important he was to those championship teams. The New England franchise was transformed when Brady came off the bench in '01 for an injured Drew Bledsoe. Receivers and running backs and coordinators have come and gone, but Brady and coach Bill Belichick have defined more than a decade of Patriots excellence.

Bradshaw, by comparison, made his entire Super Bowl run with teammates Franco Harris, Lynn Swann, John Stallworth, Mike Webster, Joe Greene, Jack Lambert, Jack Ham and Mel Blount—all Hall of Famers. And while Bradshaw was a great big-game quarterback, his career touchdown-to-interception ratio is 212–210. Brady's is 359–134.

If there is any doubt that 12 is a number for great passers, consider another one: **John Stockton**. The Jazz point guard holds the NBA's assist record by a wide margin—15,806, well ahead of Jason Kidd's 12,091.

➤ THE VERDICT
TOM BRADY

A BRIEF HISTORY OF SHORT STINTS

Grasping for history, the Rays retired number 12 for WADE BOGGS even though he only played two seasons for Tampa Bay. Boggs did grow up in Tampa and reached 3,000 hits in the franchise's second year, 1999. . . . MICHAEL JORDAN wore the number 12 for one game, on Feb. 14, 1990 in Orlando, because his signature 23 jersey had been stolen before the game. Jordan scored 49 points that night.

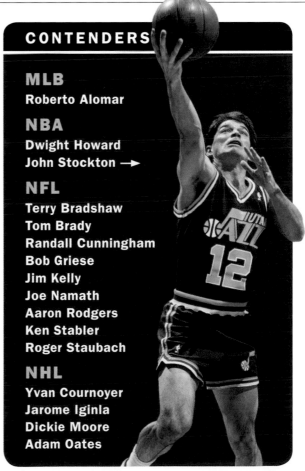

CONTENDERS

MLB
Roberto Alomar

NBA
Dwight Howard
John Stockton ➤

NFL
Terry Bradshaw
Tom Brady
Randall Cunningham
Bob Griese
Jim Kelly
Joe Namath
Aaron Rodgers
Ken Stabler
Roger Staubach

NHL
Yvan Cournoyer
Jarome Iginla
Dickie Moore
Adam Oates

13

THE NUMBER OF THE BEST

Former Rams quarterback KURT WARNER, a vocal Christian, chose 13 for his uniform number to show that he is for religion, not superstition.... STEVE NASH, a career 13, needed a new number when he was traded to the Lakers in 2012 because the number was retired for WILT CHAMBERLAIN. The soccer fan chose 10 for Diego Maradona.... What's in a name/number combo? Among the Pro Football Hall of Famers enshrined as 13 is 1920s' end GUY CHAMBERLIN.

CONTENDERS

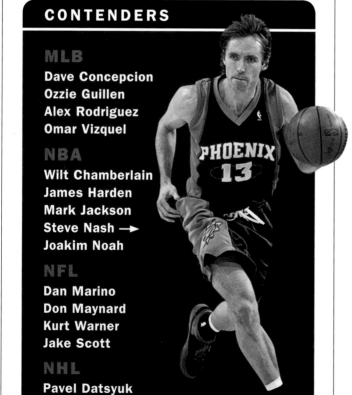

MLB
Dave Concepcion
Ozzie Guillen
Alex Rodriguez
Omar Vizquel

NBA
Wilt Chamberlain
James Harden
Mark Jackson
Steve Nash →
Joakim Noah

NFL
Dan Marino
Don Maynard
Kurt Warner
Jake Scott

NHL
Pavel Datsyuk
Mats Sundin
Ken Linseman

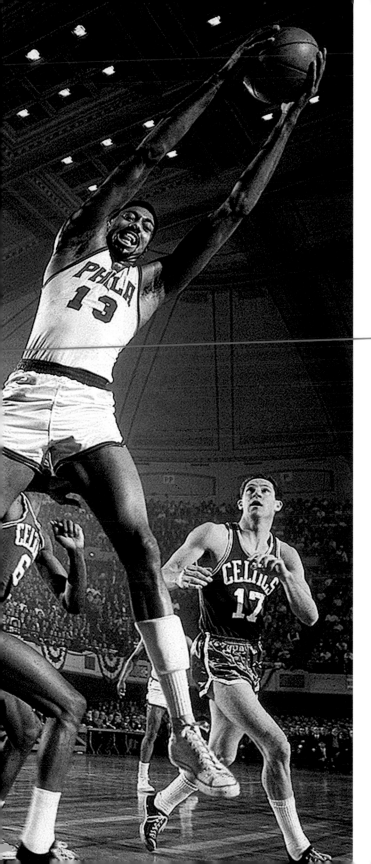

THE DEBATE

NO ONE WHO has worn the number 13 has been notably unlucky on the field of play—with the possible exception of **Ralph Branca**, the Dodgers All-Star pitcher who lives in infamy for serving up the Shot Heard 'Round the World to Bobby Thomson in 1951. But if there's a defining trait for the sports world's two top 13s, **Wilt Chamberlain** and **Dan Marino** *(below)*, it's the ability to ring up crazy stats—and few championships.

Chamberlain, the most dominant big man the NBA has ever seen, put up the gaudiest numbers of any athlete in any sport. He had a 100-point game and a 55-rebound game. In 1961–62 he averaged a league-record 50.4 points for the Philadelphia Warriors, and he also owns the next three best season scoring averages in history. In 1972–73, with the Lakers, Chamberlain's field goal percentage was .727, also an NBA record. His career rebounding average (22.9) is also the best in history. He even led the NBA in assists in '67–68, suggesting there a was a pretty good point guard hiding in that 7'1" frame.

Of course Chamberlain comes up short when it comes to championship rings: He won two (with the 76ers in 1967 and the Lakers in '72), while his rival Bill Russell, the other iconic center of the era, led the Celtics to 11. Still, Chamberlain's total is one Marino *(above)* would envy. The Hall of Fame Dolphins quarterback appeared in only one Super Bowl—and lost. His regular-season résumé is impeccable: Marino was the first quarterback to throw for 5,000 yards in a season, and he set a record with 48 touchdown passes in '84, breaking the previous mark by 12. When he retired after the '99 season he topped the career lists in completions, passing yards and touchdowns.

Marino has since had his records broken by the likes of Brady, Brees, Favre and Manning. Chamberlain's name, however, remains on top in NBA annals nearly half a century after he retired. It's easy to imagine it will remain there for a long, long time.

→ THE VERDICT

WILT CHAMBERLAIN

14

THE DEBATE

IF YOU HAD TO guess who holds the Packers franchise record for touchdown receptions, whom would you take? Sterling Sharpe? Antonio Freeman? Donald Driver? It's actually **Don Hutson**, who played in the 1930s and '40s, when the forward pass was a novelty act compared to the dominant force it is in today's NFL. Hutson led Green Bay to three titles and set every receiving record there was in a young league. Most of those records stood for decades, which is why SI football writer Peter King regards him as the greatest player ever.

And yet, Hutson barely cracks the conversation of the best to wear number 14. In basketball we have **Bob Cousy**, the great Celtics point guard of the 1950s and early '60s, and **Oscar Robertson**, who famously averaged a triple double for the Cincinnati Royals in the '61–62 season. Robertson might be the pick at 14 if he had stuck with it for his career, instead of switching to 1 when he left the Royals for the Bucks, where he won his only championship, in '70.

Instead the title goes to baseball's alltime hit king, **Pete Rose**. While Rose has been denied Hall of Fame enshrinement because he bet on baseball, there is no denying his achievements. He led the National League in hits seven times, had 10 200-hit seasons, and his final tally of 4,256 places him 67 ahead of Ty Cobb. And he electrified the sport with his 44-game hitting streak in 1978, still the longest since Joe DiMaggio's 56 in '41. Beyond that there's the undeniable charm of Charlie Hustle: He played the game like he loved it, which he undoubtedly did. Whether you believe his ban is right or wrong, it is inarguably a sad outcome.

➤ THE VERDICT
PETE ROSE

THE COOZ MEETS THE BIG O

The NBA's two greatest 14s briefly played alongside each other in 1969–70 when BOB COUSY, who had been hired to coach OSCAR ROBERTSON's Cincinnati Royals, inserted himself into the lineup, despite not having played since '63. The point guard, then 41 years old and seven years removed from his playing career, was in the lineup for only seven games— and wore 19, leaving 14 for his star scorer.

CONTENDERS

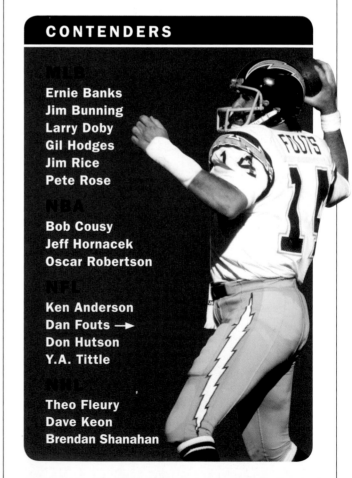

MLB
Ernie Banks
Jim Bunning
Larry Doby
Gil Hodges
Jim Rice
Pete Rose

NBA
Bob Cousy
Jeff Hornacek
Oscar Robertson

NFL
Ken Anderson
Dan Fouts ➤
Don Hutson
Y.A. Tittle

NHL
Theo Fleury
Dave Keon
Brendan Shanahan

THE DEBATE

AFTER THE DEPTH of talent at 14, the pool thins at number 15. In baseball there's **Carlos Beltran**, who will have a borderline argument for the Hall of Fame. The NBA offers up a handful of Hall of Famers from the 1950s and '60s—**Hal Greer**, **Tom Gola**, **Tom Heinsohn**—but no truly dominant figure. If we were talking about the greatest highlight by a 15, we could bring **Vince Carter** into the discussion, for his elbow-hang jam at the 2000 NBA All-Star dunk contest. But even then, that would be only the second-greatest play by a 15. The greatest belongs to the clear choice at this number, **Bart Starr**.

That play, the one-yard sneak that won the 1967 NFL title for the Packers, says a great deal about the greatness of Starr. To set the scene: It's –13° at Lambeau Field, with the windchill making it feel like –36°. Green Bay is down three points, ball on the Cowboys' one with 16 seconds left in the game, and has just used its last timeout. It is third down and Starr urges coach Vince Lombardi to run a quarterback sneak—even though, if it fails, the Packers won't have time to line up for a game-tying field goal. Lombardi approves, and the not-particularly-big Starr (6' 1", 197 pounds) crashes into the end zone behind the block of guard Jerry Kramer.

The play is exemplary because it shows the trust Lombardi had in his quarterback, and the extent to which the two were partners. It also demonstrates Starr's ability to deliver in big games. Starr's teams were 9–1 in the postseason and won five NFL championship games and the first two Super Bowls. Starr was the MVP of both, and that's more than enough to stand out in this field.

→ **THE VERDICT**

BART STARR

THE CAPTAIN'S LEGACY

The number 15 is retired by the Yankees for **THURMAN MUNSON**, who died trying to land a Cessna he was piloting in 1979. Munson, the '76 AL MVP, was the first team captain the Yankees had named since Lou Gehrig. . . . In '99 Reds manager **JACK MCKEON** wore 15 until the team acquired **DENNY NEAGLE**. For handing the number over, the pitcher thanked McKeon with a stash of stogies.

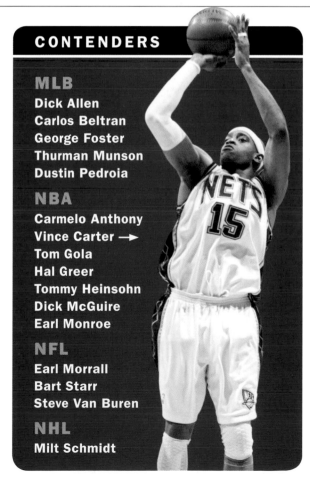

CONTENDERS

MLB
Dick Allen
Carlos Beltran
George Foster
Thurman Munson
Dustin Pedroia

NBA
Carmelo Anthony
Vince Carter →
Tom Gola
Hal Greer
Tommy Heinsohn
Dick McGuire
Earl Monroe

NFL
Earl Morrall
Bart Starr
Steve Van Buren

NHL
Milt Schmidt

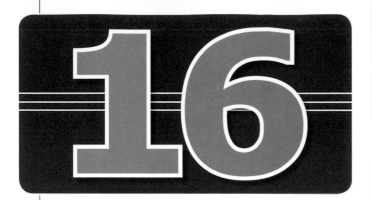

16

A DEVELOPING SITUATION

PAU GASOL **wears 16 as** a legacy from playing in his native Spain. There league roster players were given numbers 4 to 15, with 16 and 17 reserved for developmental players. Gasol asked to keep his 16 when he joined the regular roster and continued with it in the NBA. . . .

FRANK GIFFORD wore 16 even though he was a running back because when he started out in college at USC, he was a QB. He kept it when he joined the Giants, who retired the number in his honor.

CONTENDERS

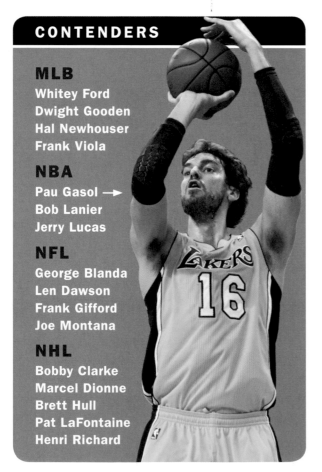

MLB
Whitey Ford
Dwight Gooden
Hal Newhouser
Frank Viola

NBA
Pau Gasol →
Bob Lanier
Jerry Lucas

NFL
George Blanda
Len Dawson
Frank Gifford
Joe Montana

NHL
Bobby Clarke
Marcel Dionne
Brett Hull
Pat LaFontaine
Henri Richard

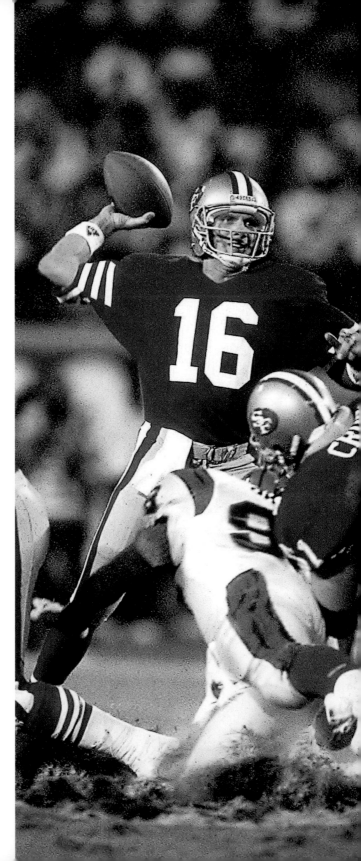

"WE'LL SHOW UP" was the quote trumpeted on the cover of SI's Super Bowl XXIV preview issue. The speaker was Broncos coach Dan Reeves, before a matchup against the 49ers that no one gave Denver a chance to win. The Broncos did indeed show up at the Superdome—and were crushed 55–10. In the competition to name the greatest 16, the architect of that rout, San Francisco quarterback **Joe Montana,** wins in a similar landslide—even though the number offers a strong collection of talent.

In football there's **Frank Gifford** (*below*), who was a star halfback for the Giants long before he married Kathie Lee. In basketball there's rebounding machine **Jerry Lucas**, and super skilled **Pau Gasol**, Kobe Bryant's sidekick for two titles with the Lakers. Hockey offers a strong contingent as a group, with Flyers center **Bobby Clarke**, of the wonderfully nicknamed Broad Street Bullies, leading the charge. Baseball has **Whitey Ford**, the Yankees' diminutive ace from the 1950s. Talented but troubled pitcher **Dwight Gooden** might have posed a threat to Montana if he had kept his nose a tad cleaner.

But to challenge Montana a player would have to prove himself a historic winner while revolutionizing the way his sport is played, as Montana did in San Francisco in Bill Walsh's West Coast offense. Montana, a third-round pick out of Notre Dame, was the perfect quarterback for Walsh. He was supremely accurate, enabling receivers to run after the catch, and he was mobile. Most of all, he was unflappable. Whether Montana was finding Dwight Clark for the Catch in the 1981 NFC championship, or was down by three in Super Bowl XXIII and pointing out John Candy in the stands before leading his team to a championship touchdown, he couldn't have been cooler under pressure. He was the greatest quarterback of his day, and of all time.

→ THE VERDICT
JOE MONTANA

17

THE DEBATE

THE HIGH TEENS are the province of many great quarterbacks, but the quality dips at number 17. The best here are players who were fine enough in their day—**Jim Hart**, **Billy Kilmer**, **Don Meredith**—but the timbers don't quite shiver at the mention of their names.

The best athlete at this number is one for whom football was the path not taken. **John Havlicek** was a star quarterback as a high-schooler in Ohio and could reportedly throw the ball 80 yards. While he chose to focus on basketball at Ohio State, and led the Buckeyes to a championship, he was still drafted by the Browns in the seventh round of the 1962 NFL draft. Cleveland tried him at wide receiver but cut him in training camp, so he reported to the NBA team that had drafted him in the first round, the Celtics. Which, to judge by history, is where he truly belonged. A guard/forward swingman, he played sixth man on six Bill Russell–led championship teams, then emerged as a starter and team leader as Boston added two more banners to the rafters in 1974 and '76. He developed into a fine scorer, averaging 20.8 points, along with 6.3 rebounds and 4.8 assists, for his career (remember, he was coming off the bench in the beginning). Just as important, he embodied the image of the perfect Celtic of the era: calm and clutch. No one hustled more than Havlicek, and he's the clear top guy here.

The second-best player at 17? How about **Jari Kurri**, who played right wing next to Wayne Gretzky for the Oilers and Kings. Kurri, a native of Finland, topped 100 points six times and was the team's leading scorer in the playoffs for all four of his and Gretzky's Stanley Cup seasons together.

➡ THE VERDICT

JOHN HAVLICEK

50

IF I COULD BE LIKE HAV. . .

There's no doubt who CHRIS MULLIN had as a role model. The Warriors forward, who won Olympic gold in 1984 as a collegian and in '92 with the Dream Team, wore 17 to honor JOHN HAVLICEK, his boyhood idol. . . . One of baseball's unwritten rules: if your name is WOODY WILLIAMS, you must wear 17. The first, a Reds infielder, wore it from 1943 to '45. The second, a pitcher, wore it for the Padres in 2005–06.

CONTENDERS

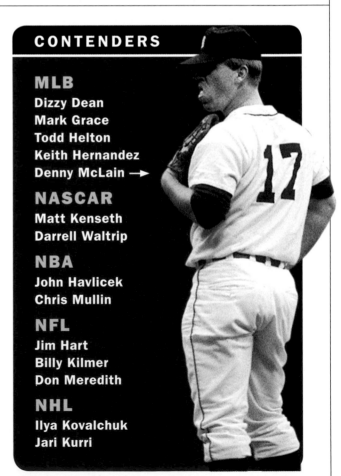

MLB
Dizzy Dean
Mark Grace
Todd Helton
Keith Hernandez
Denny McLain ➡

NASCAR
Matt Kenseth
Darrell Waltrip

NBA
John Havlicek
Chris Mullin

NFL
Jim Hart
Billy Kilmer
Don Meredith

NHL
Ilya Kovalchuk
Jari Kurri

18

DON'T GO ARCHIE IN AN ELI ZONE

For years the speed limit on Manning Way on the Ole Miss campus was 18 miles an hour, in honor of ARCHIE MANNING, but in 2012, after son Eli won his second Super Bowl, they lowered the speed limit to 10, Eli's number with the Giants and at Ole Miss.... OMRI CASSPI, the first Israeli-born NBA player, wore 18 with the Kings in 2009 because it is the numeric value of the letters in the Hebrew word *chai*, which means life. In Cleveland 18 was unavailable so he went to its double, 36.

CONTENDERS

MLB
Matt Cain
Al Cowens
Johnny Damon →
Ted Kluszewski
Don Larsen
Bret Saberhagen

NASCAR
Kyle Busch
Bobby Labonte

NBA
Dave Cowens

NFL
Charlie Joiner
Peyton Manning

NHL
Mike Ricci
Denis Savard
Serge Savard

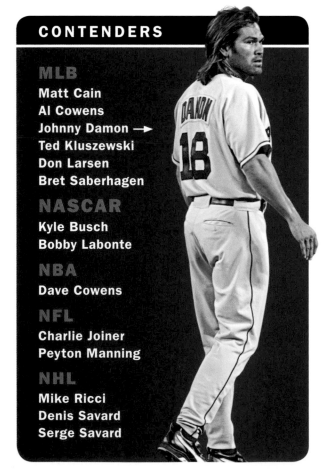

THE MOST INTERESTING quirk of the debate at 18 is the duplication of surnames among top stars. Of course there's **Peyton Manning**, who wears the same number that his father **Archie** made famous at Ole Miss. Then there are **Serge Savard** and **Denis Savard**—they are unrelated, but both were raised in the Montreal area and became hockey Hall of Famers. Next up are the Cowenses. **Dave Cowens** (*below*) starred in the frontcourt of two Celtics championship teams of the 1970s. Baseball has **Al Cowens**, the Royals outfielder who finished second in the AL MVP voting in '77, and who has obviously been dragged into this discussion only to flesh out a theme.

The choice at 18 has to be Peyton Manning. Throughout his career, if Manning has been a team's starting quarterback, you could pretty much pencil in the playoffs. After getting a 3–13 season out of the way as a rookie, he took the Colts to the postseason 11 of the next 12 years. While the team only won one Super Bowl during that time, if he was there, the team had a chance. And he was always there, starting every regular-season game plus playoffs (another 19 games) from 1998 through 2010. When he missed the '11 season with a neck injury and the Colts fell apart, dropping from 10 wins to two, it stoked an argument that perhaps Manning should win an MVP award (it would have been his fifth) because his absence underlined how valuable he was. In his first two years in Denver he won another NFL MVP and went to the Super Bowl after the 2013 season.

If there's an outsider argument to be made at 18 it would be for **Johnny Damon**, on the strength of 2,769 career hits and his role as the lovable longhair on the curse-breaking 2004 Red Sox team. But Damon had his shortcomings on defense, and he never finished higher than 13th in MVP voting. He was never an indispensable figure—not like Manning.

➤ THE VERDICT

PEYTON MANNING

19

THE DEBATE

IT WOULD BE FUN if the debate for the best 19 came down to **Robin Yount** and **Tony Gwynn**, if only as an excuse to mention that Yount had 3,142 hits, Gwynn had 3,141, and therefore Yount wins. As if the tiniest of edges in one stat was all that mattered.

But for many who wore number 19, the story goes beyond stats. There's **Willis Reed**, for example, whose limping walk onto the floor is credited with inspiring the Knicks toward the 1970 NBA title. Or **Steve Yzerman**, who was named captain of the Red Wings at the tender age of 21 and held the position for two decades as Detroit won three Stanley Cups.

But the contest for the top spot comes down to two of the more mythic figures in any sport. **Bob Feller** was a celebrity from moment he arrived in the Indians rotation at 17 years old. Rapid Robert struck out 15 in his first major league start, and later in his rookie season he fanned 17. It will be a long time before anyone strikes out his age. At 23 Feller left baseball to serve in the Navy during World War II; he returned almost four years later highly decorated and still with his fastball. For his career he had 266 wins, seven strikeout crowns, three no-hitters and a dozen one-hitters.

But the choice is **Johnny Unitas**, who had a name that sounded like it came out of a comic book, and a game that would have impressed Sun Tzu. Unitas was great not only with the arm but also between the ears, calling his own plays and directing the Colts of the late 1950s and '60s, in an era when quarterbacks were true field generals. Anyone who watched the three-time MVP and three-time NFL champion was lucky enough to see a model of a leader, and a winner.

→ THE VERDICT
JOHNNY UNITAS

SOON EVERYONE WAS DOING IT

Several years before the NFL opened up numbers 10 through 19 to receivers, KEYSHAWN JOHNSON was given an exception to wear the lower digits because in his rookie training camp with the Jets, all the 80s had been assigned to others. . . . JOE MONTANA wore 19, the number he had worn as a youngster, for his two late-career seasons in Kansas City because the Chiefs had retired number 16 for Len Dawson.

CONTENDERS

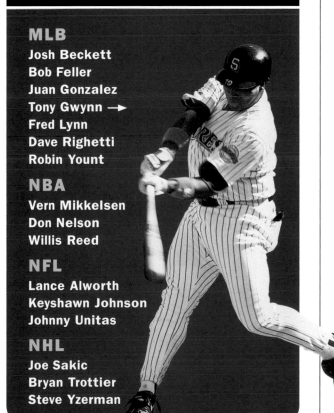

MLB
Josh Beckett
Bob Feller
Juan Gonzalez
Tony Gwynn →
Fred Lynn
Dave Righetti
Robin Yount

NBA
Vern Mikkelsen
Don Nelson
Willis Reed

NFL
Lance Alworth
Keyshawn Johnson
Johnny Unitas

NHL
Joe Sakic
Bryan Trottier
Steve Yzerman

NBA

BY THE NUMBERS

What jersey has the richest history at each position? If you were to build a team by numbers, these are the digits you'd want to draft at each spot

POINT GUARD 1

Chauncey Billups, Baron Davis, Anfernee Hardaway, Oscar Robertson, Gus Williams

Next best: 3 (Dennis Johnson, Stephon Marbury, Chris Paul)

SHOOTING GUARD 44

George Gervin, Pete Maravich, Jerry West

Next best: 24 (Kobe Bryant, Sam Jones, Reggie Theus) and 3 (Dale Ellis, Allen Iverson, Dwyane Wade)

SMALL FORWARD 33

Larry Bird, Danny Granger, Grant Hill, Scottie Pippen

Next best: 6 (Walter Davis, Julius Erving, LeBron James)

POWER FORWARD 32

Dale Davis, Karl Malone, Kevin McHale

Next best: 21 (Tim Duncan, Kevin Garnett, David West) and 11 (Harry Galatin, Elvin Hayes, Bob McAdoo)

CENTER 33

Kareem Abdul-Jabbar, Patrick Ewing, Alonzo Mourning

Next best: 34 (Mel Daniels, Hakeem Olajuwon, Shaquille O'Neal)

Most Worn **12**
357 players have had it. Most notable: John Stockton

Least Worn *15 numbers have never been used:*
58, 59, 63, 64, 69, 74, 75, 78, 79, 80, 81, 82, 87, 95, 97

Most MVPs **33**
A total of nine: six for Abdul-Jabbar, three for Bird

Most Finals MVPs **23, 34**
Six each—all Jordan at 23, three players at 34

Most Retired **32**
Nine teams have hung it up

Scottie Pippen

20

DETROIT'S GREATEST MODEL NUMBER

BARRY SANDERS **is the** greatest, but not the only, Lion to bring glory in number 20. BILLY SIMS, the first overall pick in 1980 out of Oklahoma, enjoyed three 1,000-yard seasons and was named to three Pro Bowls before a knee injury ended his career. Before Sims there was cornerback LEM BARNEY, a Hall of Famer who played from '67 to '77. Barney was electric with his hands on the ball. He scored 11 career touchdowns, seven on interception runs and four on special teams returns.

CONTENDERS

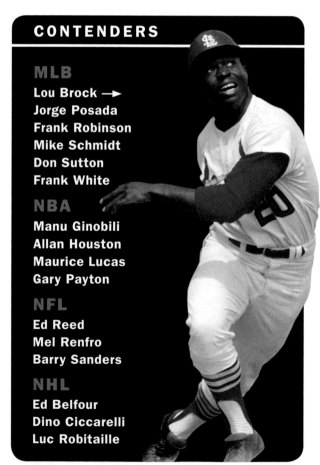

MLB

Lou Brock →
Jorge Posada
Frank Robinson
Mike Schmidt
Don Sutton
Frank White

NBA

Manu Ginobili
Allan Houston
Maurice Lucas
Gary Payton

NFL

Ed Reed
Mel Renfro
Barry Sanders

NHL

Ed Belfour
Dino Ciccarelli
Luc Robitaille

THE DEBATE

IN THESE apples-to-oranges comparisons it can be fun to imagine athletes from different sports taking each other on directly, and none more so than here. **Gary Payton** and **Mike Schmidt** *(below)* were both outstanding defensive players in their respective sports. But were they so great at defense that they could have stopped **Barry Sanders**?

It's hard to imagine they could, and not just because neither Payton nor Schmidt really had a frame for football. No one who looked at home in shoulder pads could stop the Lions running back either. His name remains synonymous with a kind of speedy, shifty running that, it seems, contemporary backs like LeSean McCoy can reference but never duplicate. A couple of moves and Sanders would have defenders going this way and that, spinning around, not knowing which way to turn. Sometimes it didn't even take that long—Sanders had them psyched out before he stepped on the field. In a 1994 SI story Bears defenders spoke of experiencing sleepless nights before they played Detroit. "You sit up in  the middle of the night hollering, 'Barry! Sanders!' " said defensive tackle Henry Thomas. Sanders is all the more intriguing because he retired after 10 NFL seasons at age 31, showing an indifference to all the records he might have owned if he had carried on. His greatest statistical season came in '97, when he ran for 2,053 yards (a 128.3 per game average, and an insane 6.1 yards per attempt). The next season, an average one by his standards, he gained 1,491 yards. Then he was gone.

Schmidt offers Sanders his stiffest competition. The Phillies' third baseman is a reminder of what offense in baseball was like in the '70s and '80s. Though sometimes with unremarkable totals, the three-time MVP led the majors in home runs for eight seasons. He showed impressive range in the field too, winning 10 Gold Gloves. Schmidt may be the most complete third baseman ever, but it is Sanders's magic that gives him the edge.

➤ **THE VERDICT**

BARRY SANDERS

21

THE DEBATE

WELCOME TO the 21 Club, which is packed with some of the biggest personalities in sports. The Human Highlight Film, **Dominique Wilkins**, is here, as is **Roger Clemens**, who wore the number when he was dominating batters with the Red Sox and Blue Jays (though not when he was throwing shards of bat at them with the Yankees). The most virtuous member of the club is **Roberto Clemente**, who racked up 3,000 hits with the Pirates and became a cultural icon for his humanitarian work, dying tragically in a 1972 crash while flying to Nicaragua to deliver earthquake relief. Then there's **Deion Sanders**—Neon Deion, Prime Time—who defined the term shutdown corner and was as dynamic a player as the NFL has ever seen in the open field. Sanders is the biggest personality, and he would be the best player at 21 too if it weren't for **Tim Duncan**.

The introverted Spurs center avoids the limelight as earnestly as Sanders high-stepped toward it. The only subtly showy element of his game is the way he banks shots off the glass, a lost art. But the choice is Duncan because he has been too good for too long—17 NBA seasons and counting. He won two titles alongside David Robinson, and three more with Tony Parker and Manu Ginobili. He and coach Gregg Popovich are the NBA analog of Tom Brady and Bill Belichick, defining the culture of a franchise, creating an environment in which players come and go and the machine hums along. Sanders was almost the opposite in this regard—he popped into San Francisco and Dallas and brought the championship topping to what were already excellent teams. But Duncan is the foundation.

➤ THE VERDICT
TIM DUNCAN

THEY CAN'T HAVE IT ALL

The last quarterback ever to wear number 21 was JOHN HADL, who played from 1962 to '77. He was grandfathered in after the NFL limited quarterbacks to numbers 19 and lower in '73. . . . KEVIN GARNETT wore 21 in Minnesota, but switched to 5 when he was traded the Celtics. His number was among the 21 numbers that were already retired and hanging from the rafters in Boston.

CONTENDERS

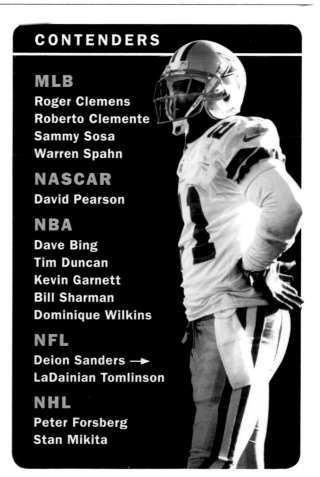

MLB
Roger Clemens
Roberto Clemente
Sammy Sosa
Warren Spahn

NASCAR
David Pearson

NBA
Dave Bing
Tim Duncan
Kevin Garnett
Bill Sharman
Dominique Wilkins

NFL
Deion Sanders ➤
LaDainian Tomlinson

NHL
Peter Forsberg
Stan Mikita

THE DEBATE

HERE WE ARE awash in excellence. Consider these top contenders from each sport. In baseball, it's **Jim Palmer**, who had not just beautiful hair, but eight 20-win seasons, a career ERA of 2.86 and three Cy Young awards. His Orioles teams appeared in six World Series, winning three.

In the NHL we have **Mike Bossy**, who, along with Wayne Gretzky, had more 50-goal seasons than any player in history, and won four Stanley Cups for the Islanders. In basketball, the man is **Elgin Baylor**, narrowly over **Clyde Drexler**. Baylor and his Lakers never won an NBA championship, often meeting Finals frustration at the hands of Bill Russell and the Celtics. (If Baylor and the Glide commiserated, Baylor might express frustration that Russell never took a couple years off to play baseball the way Michael Jordan had, thus creating a window for Drexler to get his ring.)

The choice, though, is **Emmitt Smith**. He gained renown as one of the "Triplets," along with Troy Aikman and Michael Irvin, who led the Cowboys to three Super Bowl wins in the early 1990s. But among this trio, Smith stands out. He is the NFL's career leader in rushing (by 1,629 yards, ahead of Walter Payton) and rushing touchdowns (by 19, ahead of LaDainian Tomlinson). He was a master at picking up blitzes, and he played through pain, racking up 229 total yards in the 1993 season finale while playing with a separated shoulder. It's common to theorize that certain players are overrated because they played on such loaded teams that the defense couldn't focus on just them. Smith might actually be underrated after playing alongside two camera-ready stars. Here he stands supreme.

➤ THE VERDICT
EMMITT SMITH

MY NUMBER'S ON THE CHECK

In 2007, anticipating the return of ROGER CLEMENS from retirement, Yankees second baseman ROBINSON CANO switched his number from 22 to 24 before the season began. Clemens did return and reclaim his number, dramatically: He announced his comeback to the crowd at Yankee Stadium during a seventh-inning stretch. His new contract was a prorated deal for $28,000,022.

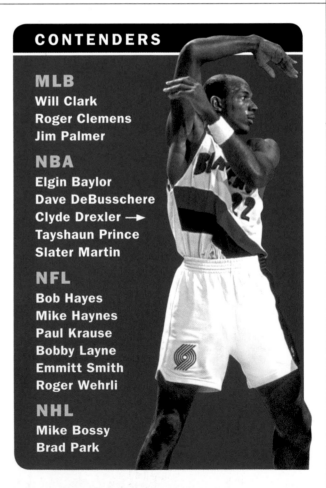

CONTENDERS

MLB
Will Clark
Roger Clemens
Jim Palmer

NBA
Elgin Baylor
Dave DeBusschere
Clyde Drexler ➤
Tayshaun Prince
Slater Martin

NFL
Bob Hayes
Mike Haynes
Paul Krause
Bobby Layne
Emmitt Smith
Roger Wehrli

NHL
Mike Bossy
Brad Park

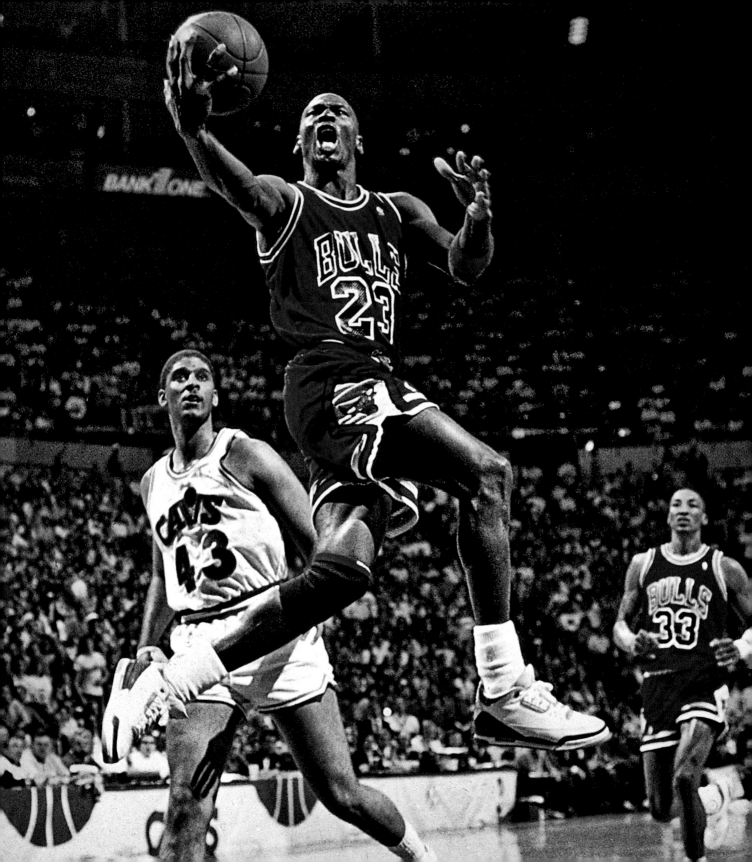

THE DEBATE

WHAT IS IT about the number 23 and Chicago? You could argue that three of the top seven 23s made their bones there—upping that total if you really loved **Robin Ventura** and his years with the White Sox. At number seven on the list you have **Devin Hester**, the most dangerous return man in NFL history, with 18 touchdowns and immeasurable yards of field position gained from punters whom he intimidates into kicking the ball out-of-bounds. Some non-Chicagoans follow—**Calvin Murphy**, **Don Mattingly**, **David Beckham** (the Real Madrid years) and **LeBron James** (in Cleveland)—and then at the runner-up spot is **Ryne Sandberg**, the best Cub since Ernie Banks. The slugging second baseman led the National League in home runs one year, triples in another. He had a 200-hit season, a 54-steal season and won nine straight Gold Gloves. He did everything but win the big one.

Speaking of winning . . . **Michael Jordan**. He is so synonymous with winning that it's easy to forget he didn't reach the NBA Finals until his seventh season. For a while it looked like he might be known only as a scorer and highlight star. But in time Jordan proved himself the most relentless winner in sports, in a narrow group that might also include Tiger Woods in his prime. Jordan won titles and MVP awards and he was named defensive player of the year, but what defined his game was the way he finished. If the Bulls were within striking distance or, God forbid, a little bit ahead, he did what it took to finish the job. It might be a pass to Steve Kerr, it might be a steal from Karl Malone and a shot over Bryon Russell. Whatever. He owned the last two minutes, and he owns number 23.

THE VERDICT
MICHAEL JORDAN

IN TRIBUTE TO HIS AIRNESS

Before he joined the Heat and dropped 23 for the number 6, LEBRON JAMES said that the NBA should retire 23 leaguewide to honor Jordan. . . . When DAVID BECKHAM came to Real Madrid the number 7 he had worn for Manchester United was taken, so he jumped to 23 as a nod to Jordan, saying he admired "everything that he represented—everything that he did in his career."

CONTENDERS

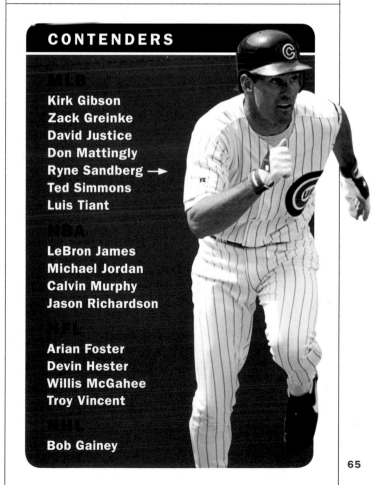

MLB

Kirk Gibson
Zack Greinke
David Justice
Don Mattingly
Ryne Sandberg →
Ted Simmons
Luis Tiant

NBA

LeBron James
Michael Jordan
Calvin Murphy
Jason Richardson

NFL

Arian Foster
Devin Hester
Willis McGahee
Troy Vincent

NHL

Bob Gainey

THE DEBATE

IN BASKETBALL you could have an amazing starting five of number 24s, starring **Sam Jones**, **Bill Bradley**, the late-career **Kobe Bryant**, **Rick Barry**, and young **Moses Malone**. (If you think such a team might be light on rebounding, you never saw the young Malone clean the glass.) In football you could put together a heck of a defensive secondary, featuring three Hall of Famers (**Willie Brown**, **Jack Christiansen**, and **Willie Wood**) and two contemporary players, **Champ Bailey** and **Darrelle Revis**, who might actually raise their standard of play.

But this number really belongs to baseball. Its wearers include 2012 Triple Crown winner **Miguel Cabrera**, alltime leading base stealer **Rickey Henderson** (he wore the number with six teams), **Ken Griffey Jr.** in his Seattle years, and the young and slim **Barry Bonds** in Pittsburgh. Of course, Bonds could not continue wearing 24 when he signed with the Giants because the franchise had retired it for the ultimate 24, **Willie Mays**.

Mays was the rare player who can be equally appreciated by the most hard-boiled sabermetrician and the most wide-eyed five-year-old boy. He had the dazzle of a star (see: *catch*, *Vic Wertz*) and the consistent production to back it up, with 660 home runs, 3,283 hits and 12 Gold Gloves. And his love for the game was evident. He would hit a home run at the Polo Grounds in an afternoon game, and then come home and hit another homer playing stickball with the neighborhood kids as the sun came down. It's why so many great players have been inspired to wear his number, but the honor of best 24 still goes to the original.

→ **THE VERDICT**
WILLIE MAYS

WE HAVE A SPLIT DECISION. . . .

Though he won three NBA titles wearing 8 and playing with Shaquille O'Neal, KOBE BRYANT says he would prefer that the Lakers retire his number 24. Since switching to that jersey in 2006, he has won two championships. . . . RICK BARRY wanted 24 when he joined the Rockets late in his career but the number was taken by MOSES MALONE, so Barry wore 2 at home and 4 on the road.

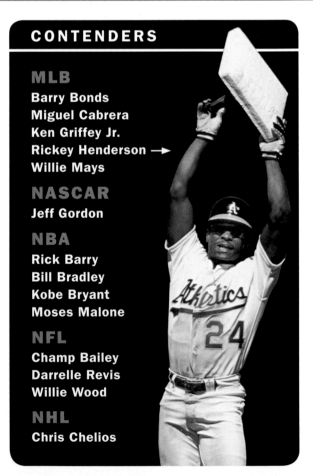

CONTENDERS

MLB
Barry Bonds
Miguel Cabrera
Ken Griffey Jr.
Rickey Henderson →
Willie Mays

NASCAR
Jeff Gordon

NBA
Rick Barry
Bill Bradley
Kobe Bryant
Moses Malone

NFL
Champ Bailey
Darrelle Revis
Willie Wood

NHL
Chris Chelios

25

FOLLOWING IN THEIR FOOTSTEPS

While gaining fame as a wide receiver, FRED BILETNIKOFF wore a running back's number because when he arrived at Florida State, that was his position. He chose 25 to honor his boyhood idol, running back TOMMY MCDONALD. Biletnikoff eventually joined McDonald in the Pro Football Hall of Fame. . . . DOC RIVERS wore 25 as a point guard for 13 seasons. Now his son AUSTIN is carrying on the family tradition in New Orleans.

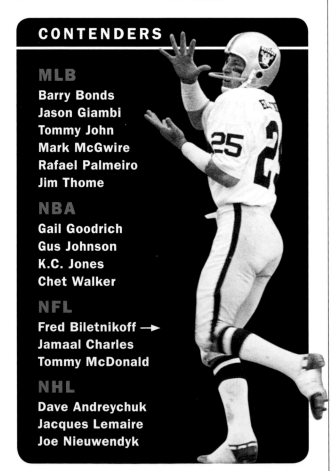

CONTENDERS

MLB

Barry Bonds
Jason Giambi
Tommy John
Mark McGwire
Rafael Palmeiro
Jim Thome

NBA

Gail Goodrich
Gus Johnson
K.C. Jones
Chet Walker

NFL

Fred Biletnikoff →
Jamaal Charles
Tommy McDonald

NHL

Dave Andreychuk
Jacques Lemaire
Joe Nieuwendyk

IS 25 THE mark of a cheat? It's ridiculous, of course, to ascribe such properties to an integer, and it's equally obvious that many outstanding athletes who wore the number played with honor. But still . . .

In football, for instance, the greatest 25 is **Fred Biletnikoff**, a Raiders wideout and notable user of the most notorious performance-enhancing substance of his day: Stickum, an adhesive goo that receivers rubbed on their hands to help them make catches. Two years after Biletnikoff retired in 1978, the NFL banned Stickum, but he still made it to the Hall of Fame.

Other 25s may not be so en-  shrined. Two players are recognizable as much for their appearances at a congressional hearing as for what they did on the diamond. **Mark McGwire** (*right*, 583 home runs), was not there to talk about the past when he appeared on Capitol Hill in 2005 to testify about steroid use. That same day, **Rafael Palmeiro** (569 home runs) declared under oath, finger pointed, that he had never used steroids. Five months later Major League Baseball suspended him for failing a drug test. **Jason Giambi** (438 home runs), who did not appear in Washington, admitted to using performance enhancers. Another who has denied knowingly taking PEDs but who remains the poster boy for a regrettable era is **Barry Bonds** (762 home runs). Bonds wore 24 for the first seven years of his career with Pittsburgh. But it was in San Francisco, while wearing 25, that his home run totals increased in correspondence with his hat size. Still, what Bonds did was mind-boggling. He won four consecutive MVP awards from '01 to '04. He broke Hank Aaron's career home run record, and his career OPS is the fourth-best of all time, behind only Babe Ruth, Ted Williams and Lou Gehrig. Call him a cheater, call him a product of his time, call him both. He is the only choice to represent number 25.

→ THE VERDICT

BARRY BONDS

26

THE DEBATE

"LOTS OF CHICKEN and sex addiction" is not the premise of a new reality show on A&E—not yet, anyway—but the phrase encapsulates what the casual fan may remember about **Wade Boggs**. First he became known as the guy who ate chicken before every game. Then, in 1989, amid a scandal sparked by the revelation of his extramarital affair, he did a TV interview in which he announced that he was a sex addict—which most people didn't know was a thing until Boggs brought it into the public arena.

He's our man at 26, not for any of the above, but for the reasons anyone cared about his personal business in the first place. In his prime, while Boggs was wearing the number (he ditched it when he left Boston for New York and Tampa Bay), he was a master at work. Look at his run from 1983 to '89, when he reeled off seven 200-hit seasons in a row, including 240 hits in '85. For six of those seven seasons he led the majors in on-base percentage as well. Boggs wasn't much of a power threat, with 118 career homers, and he was even less dangerous on the bases, with only 24 steals. That last stat also tells you he wasn't beating out a ton of grounders, and this underlines how good he was at hitting 'em where they ain't.

Boggs is a narrow choice over the outstanding **Rod Woodson**. Adept at tackling and coverage, he made All-Pro as a cornerback and later as a safety. He was also a dangerous returner, making All-Pro at that position as well, before coaches decided he was too valuable to risk that way. The 1993 Defensive Player of the Year is a clean second, ahead of speedy Packers cover corner **Herb Adderley**.

➤ THE VERDICT

WADE BOGGS

LOOKING FOR A CUT RATE

After being traded from Denver to Washington, running back CLINTON PORTIS promised Redskins defensive back Ifeanyi Ohalete $40,000 for the right to wear 26—and paid him a first installment of $20,000. But then Ohalete was cut in camp, and Portis refused to pay the rest. Ohalete took him to court, and they eventually settled on Portis's paying $18,000 of the remainder.

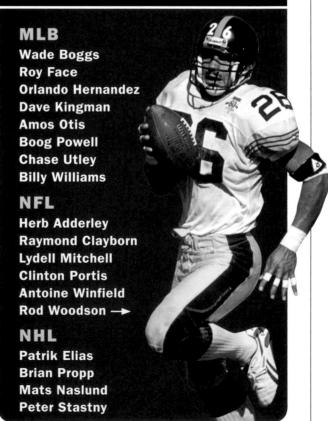

CONTENDERS

MLB
Wade Boggs
Roy Face
Orlando Hernandez
Dave Kingman
Amos Otis
Boog Powell
Chase Utley
Billy Williams

NFL
Herb Adderley
Raymond Clayborn
Lydell Mitchell
Clinton Portis
Antoine Winfield
Rod Woodson ➤

NHL
Patrik Elias
Brian Propp
Mats Naslund
Peter Stastny

27

THE NUMBER OF THE ANGELS

Not to get ahead of ourselves, but it's possible that two of the greatest hitters to wear the Angels uniform have shared a number. VLADIMIR GUERRERO, the 2004 AL MVP, wore 27 from '04 to '09. Now comes MIKE TROUT, who in 2012 won Rookie of the Year and finished second in the MVP voting. . . . Sibling act: A decade after CALDWELL JONES wore 27 with the Rockets, brother CHARLES JONES also wore the number in Houston.

CONTENDERS

MLB
Kevin Brown
Carlton Fisk
Vladimir Guerrero
Catfish Hunter
Matt Kemp
Juan Marichal
Scott Rolen
Mike Trout

NBA
Jack Twyman

NFL
Steve Atwater
Eddie George →
Ken Houston
Ray Rice

NHL
Frank Mahovlich
Scott Niedermayer
Darryl Sittler

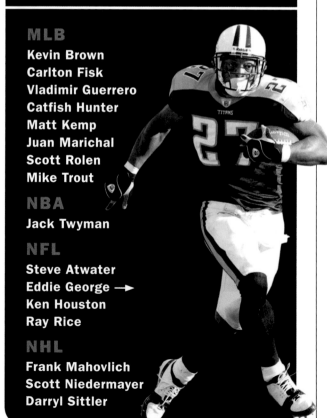

HE IS BEST remembered for his days with the Red Sox, with whom he was named AL Rookie of the Year in 1972, made seven All-Star teams and waved an iconic home run fair in what is easily the most famous October blast by a player whose team ended up losing the World Series. And while **Carlton Fisk** *(below)* was with the Red Sox, he wore 27.

Then he went to the White Sox and had to switch his uniform number to 72. Fisk actually played longer in Chicago, from '81 to '93, than he did in Boston. His greatest home run season was also in Chicago (37, in '85) as was his highest finish in an MVP race (third, in 1983). Still, if *Good Will Hunting* had been set at Northwestern instead of at Harvard, Matt Damon and Robin Williams wouldn't have been talking about Carlton Fisk in their therapy sessions. (Would they have been talking about Leon Durham?)

If Fisk had stayed with 27 he would be the choice, but his flip-flop creates an opening for **Juan Marichal**, who wore 27 for all of his 14 seasons with the Giants, only abandoning the number—irony alert—when he joined the Red Sox for a season in 1974 and found it was in use by a certain catcher.

Marichal had done his career's work long before then. He had an elegant pitching motion but was also a workhorse, throwing an amazing 244 complete games—more games than he actually won (243). Of course it was a different time, as demonstrated by the most amazing game Marichal pitched, which is also a contender for the greatest regular-season game ever. In 1963 the young Marichal dueled the Braves' Warren Spahn in a 16-inning game that ended 1–0, with both pitchers going the distance. Marichal threw 16 shutout innings against a lineup that included Hank Aaron and Eddie Mathews. Pretty astounding. If *Good Will Hunting* were set in San Francisco, maybe Damon and Williams would have been talking about that.

➤ THE VERDICT
JUAN MARICHAL

28

THE DEBATE

THIS IS WHY Halls of Fame employ waiting periods. It's nearly impossible to judge a career that is long done against one that's still playing out on *SportsCenter*. There is no doubt that **Adrian Peterson** is the best running back in the NFL today. He's fast enough to get to the edge, and strong enough to break tackles up the middle. Watch him now and it's hard to imagine anyone better at the position.

But here's a fact for you: Not once has Peterson had as many yards from scrimmage as **Marshall Faulk** had in his best year. In 2012, when Peterson carried an otherwise middling Vikings team into the playoffs, he had 2,314 yards from scrimmage, with 2,097 yards rushing. Faulk, in 1999, had 2,429 yards from scrimmage, but what's really impressive is that he achieved that total with 1,381 yards rushing and 1,048 yards receiving. You know how they say that an SAT score is more impressive when the math and verbal are close to each other? It's the same thing here, because it marks Faulk as a transformative back, the kind who could dominate when the ball was on the ground *and* in the air. With the Rams he helped keep the Greatest Show on Turf running as it won the Super Bowl in 2000 and played for a second championship two years later.

While there are many great backs at this number, the next man on the list is **Darrell Green**, who may have been speedier than all of them. The Redskins' cornerback announced his presence as a rookie when he ran down Tony Dorsett from behind in a Monday night game. Dorsett was the first of many to hear the 5' 9" Green's footsteps. He played in Washington for two decades, losing remarkably few steps along the way.

➤ **THE VERDICT**
MARSHALL FAULK

A PRICE BELOW RUBIES

Here's a story about a number being sold for two cases of beer. The players involved were, predictably, JOHN KRUK and MITCH WILLIAMS. In explaining his easy sale to the team's new reliever in 1991, Kruk told *The New York Times*, "The only reason Mitch wanted the number is because his wife had a lot of number 28 jewelry and he didn't want to buy her any more jewelry. Not long after that, he got divorced and changed numbers."

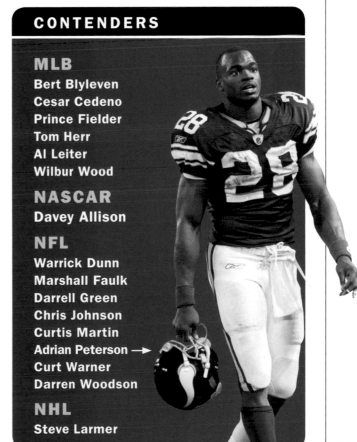

CONTENDERS

MLB
Bert Blyleven
Cesar Cedeno
Prince Fielder
Tom Herr
Al Leiter
Wilbur Wood

NASCAR
Davey Allison

NFL
Warrick Dunn
Marshall Faulk
Darrell Green
Chris Johnson
Curtis Martin
Adrian Peterson →
Curt Warner
Darren Woodson

NHL
Steve Larmer

29

THE DEBATE

THERE ARE three contenders with extremely strong arguments to be the best number 29. First, there's **Rod Carew**, who accumulated batting titles at a faster clip than anyone in recent history, winning seven between 1969 and '78. In his most memorable seasons he threatened to become the first player to hit .400 since Ted Williams. Carew's best run at it came in '77, when he hit .388. In '83, at age 37, he carried a .443 average into June. Carew leveled out that year, winding up with a .339 average. Still, it was his 15th consecutive season hitting above .300.

While Carew never reached the hitter's holy grail, **Eric Dickerson** created a statistical target for other running backs to shoot for. In 1984 he ran for 2,105 yards for the Los Angeles Rams. Since then others—Barry Sanders, Chris Johnson and Adrian Peterson, to name a few—have come close to that total, but no one has topped the mark. Dickerson's big season wasn't an anomaly. He won four NFL rushing titles and reached the 10,000 yard mark faster than any other back (91 games).

But the nod here goes to **Ken Dryden**. Few athletes have packed as much achievement into so short a career. Dryden started fast—the Canadiens made the goalie a late-season call-up in 1971 and he led them to the Stanley Cup and was named playoffs MVP the season *before* he was named Rookie of the Year—and he never slowed down, winning five more titles with Montreal before retiring after eight NHL seasons. Dryden was 31 when he quit hockey to pursue his other interests: writing, lawyering, politics. (In 2002, SI named his 1983 book *The Game* the ninth-best sports book of all time.) Dryden's career was brief, but his star still shines brightest here.

→ THE VERDICT
KEN DRYDEN

CALL IT THE TEXAS 29-STEP

Adrian Peterson and ERIC DICKERSON are both tall running backs who hail from Texas. They're also both really, really good, so it's understandable that as a young man Peterson heard himself compared with Dickerson early and often. After Peterson was drafted by the Vikings in 2007 he asked to wear Dickerson's number 29, but it wasn't available so he stayed with his old Oklahoma number, 28.

CONTENDERS

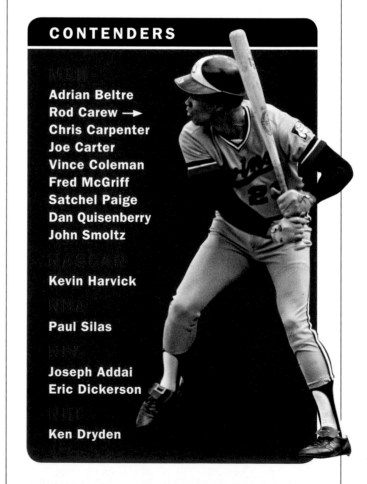

MLB
Adrian Beltre
Rod Carew →
Chris Carpenter
Joe Carter
Vince Coleman
Fred McGriff
Satchel Paige
Dan Quisenberry
John Smoltz

NASCAR
Kevin Harvick

NBA
Paul Silas

NFL
Joseph Addai
Eric Dickerson

NHL
Ken Dryden

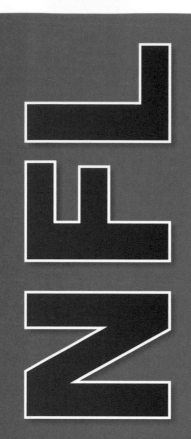

NFL

BY THE NUMBERS

What jersey has the richest history at each position? If you were to build a team by numbers, these are the digits you'd want to draft at each spot

QUARTERBACK 12

Terry Bradshaw, Tom Brady, Bob Griese, Aaron Rodgers, Ken Stabler, Roger Staubach
Next best: 16 (George Blanda, Len Dawson, Joe Montana)

RUNNING BACK 32

Marcus Allen, Jim Brown, Franco Harris, Edgerrin James, O.J. Simpson
Next best: 34 (Earl Campbell, Walter Payton, Thurman Thomas)

FULLBACK 44

Tom Rathman, John Riggins, Vonta Leach
Next best: 39 (Larry Csonka, Sam Cunningham)

WIDE RECEIVER 80

Isaac Bruce, Cris Carter, Cris Collinsworth, Steve Largent, James Lofton, Jerry Rice
Next best: 88 (Marvin Harrison, Michael Irvin, Lynn Swann)

TIGHT END 88

Tony Gonzalez, Keith Jackson, John Mackey, Riley Odoms, Charlie Sanders
Next best: 80 (Jimmy Graham, Kellen Winslow)
and 82 (Ozzie Newsome, Jason Witten)

OFFENSIVE LINEMAN 78

Anthony Muñoz, Art Shell, Jackie Slater
Next best: 73 (Larry Allen, John Hannah, Mark May, Ron Yary) and 75 (Forrest Gregg, Jonathan Ogden, Stan Walters)

DEFENSIVE LINEMAN 75

Joe Greene, Deacon Jones, Howie Long, Vince Wilfork
Next best: 74 (Henry Jordan, Bob Lilly, Merlin Olsen)

LINEBACKER 56

Hardy Nickerson, Joe Schmidt, Lawrence Taylor, Andre Tippett
Next best: 52 (Ray Lewis, Clay Matthews, Patrick Willis)

DEFENSIVE BACK 24

Champ Bailey, Willie Brown, Jack Christiansen, Ty Law, Darrelle Revis, Willie Wood

Next best: 26 (Herb Adderley, Antoine Winfield, Rod Woodson)

KICKER 3

Al Del Greco, Pete Gogolak, Stephen Gostkowski, Eddie Murray, Jan Stenerud

Next best: 4 (Jason Hanson, John Kasay, Adam Vinatieri)

PUNTER 8

Ray Guy, Brian Moorman

Next best: 4 (Bryan Barker, Andy Lee, Reggie Roby) and 2 (Darren Bennett, Dustin Colquitt, Mike Horan)

Most Worn   **83**

488 different players have sported

Least Worn   **00**

Jim Otto, Ken Burrough . . . and that's it

Most MVPs   **12**

There have been seven—all quarterbacks

Most Super Bowl MVPs   **12**

Five QBs have combined for seven trophies

Most Retired 7, 12, 40, 70

A tie at the top: Each retired by five teams

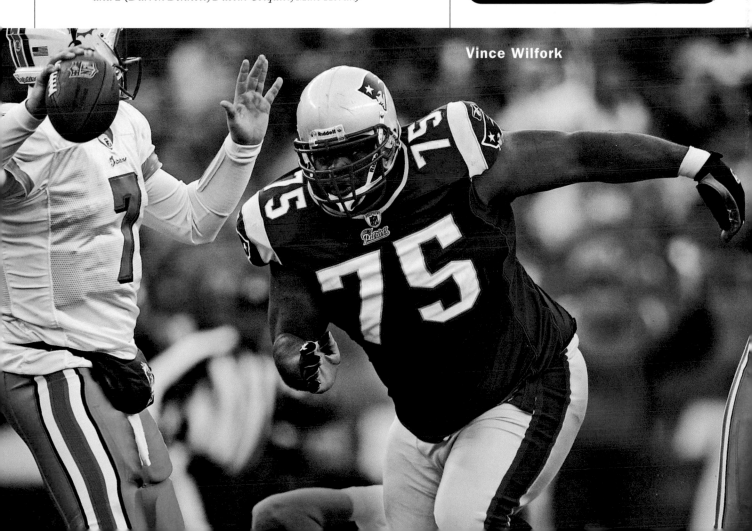

Vince Wilfork

30

THE DEBATE

IT'S TOUGH TO get to **Nolan Ryan**'s number and not choose him. He is the archetypal power pitcher, the living, breathing, Texas-born-and-bred epitome of country hardball. Ryan and his 100-mph fastball struck out more batters (5,714) than any pitcher in history and he threw an astounding seven no-hitters, another record. The Ryan Express chugged along for 26 major league seasons, and he was ornery til the end. Just ask Robin Ventura, the White Sox third baseman who charged the mound after taking exception to some of Ryan's inside heat. The 46-year-old Ryan put Ventura, who was 20 years his junior, in a headlock and wrestled him into submission. Ryan is not the greatest pitcher ever. But no one has had a more dominating presence.

Still, Ryan is second best here, and it's not because he only wore number 30 for four Mets seasons and eight Angels seasons, donning 34 the rest of the time. Even comparing their full careers, the choice would be **Martin Brodeur**. The Devils goaltender is the pick because he may well be the greatest ever at his position. He has the most career wins, by a good distance over Patrick Roy. (If a Ryan advocate were to pop in here and point out that Brodeur also holds the record for losses—well, the strikeout king also holds the major league record for walks.) Brodeur has the most shutouts too, taking the record from Terry Sawchuk. In his 19 full seasons Brodeur's New Jersey teams have made the playoffs 16 times and won three Stanley Cups. For nearly two decades Brodeur was the rock of a franchise. And he has achieved historic success while maintaining a relatively easy spirit, which only make his claim on the number stronger.

➤ **THE VERDICT**
MARTIN BRODEUR

BORROWING FROM YOUR DAD

When KEN GRIFFEY JR., joined the Reds, his father's old team, in 2000, he changed his number from 24—Cincinnati had retired it for Tony Perez—to 30, which was KEN GRIFFEY SR.'s number when he was Perez's teammate in the 1970s. . . . Sharpshooting guard STEPHEN CURRY wears number 30 for the Warriors, just as his dad DELL CURRY did with five NBA teams, most notably the Hornets.

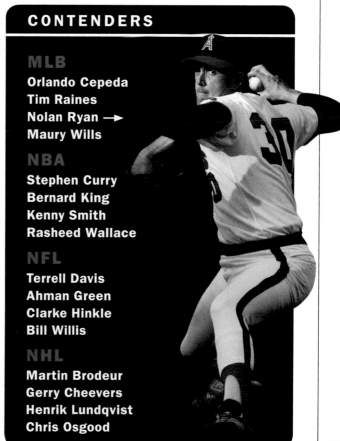

CONTENDERS

MLB
Orlando Cepeda
Tim Raines
Nolan Ryan ➤
Maury Wills

NBA
Stephen Curry
Bernard King
Kenny Smith
Rasheed Wallace

NFL
Terrell Davis
Ahman Green
Clarke Hinkle
Bill Willis

NHL
Martin Brodeur
Gerry Cheevers
Henrik Lundqvist
Chris Osgood

31

THE DEBATE

DO YOU REMEMBER the 1990s—the dotcom boom, grunge music, "I did not have sex with that woman" and all that? Some of the most memorable sports moments were provided by men wearing number 31. First, **Reggie Miller**, who in '94 went nuts on the Knicks in the playoffs, dropping 25 points in the fourth quarter of a game at Madison Square Garden, trash-talking with courtside fixture Spike Lee all the while. The next year Miller again made the Garden his personal playground, scoring eight points in the final 16.9 seconds of Game 1 of the Eastern Conference semis to lead Indiana to an amazing comeback win. For those epic moments—and for the entirety of his Hall of Fame career—Miller is a strong contender at 31.

If you look at the broader record, though, **Greg Maddux** is the clear choice. Maddux defined the elite level for righthanded pitchers—in any era. His most mind-boggling stretch was from 1992 to '95, when he won four consecutive Cy Young Awards. (His 1.56 ERA in 1994 is the third-lowest for any pitcher in the live-ball era.) Maddux was good at everything, with the notable exception of making a show of how good he was. He dominated not with radar-gun readings but with masterly control, and a mind that could outthink Big Blue. He never led the league in strikeouts, and his fastball often clocked in the 80s, but three times he led the majors in strikeout-to-walk ratio, including an 8.85-to-1 mark in 1997 that was the fifth-best of the last 125 years. There were moments in Manhattan when the loquacious Miller looked like a world-beater. But over his 23-year career, Maddux quietly proved himself to be an alltime great.

→ THE VERDICT

GREG MADDUX

THE CUBS' LUCKY NUMBER?

Two Cubs have worn number 31 and made it to the Hall of Fame—FERGUSON JENKINS, who won the Cy Young in 1971, and GREG MADDUX, who pitched in Chicago for seven years before signing with Atlanta. (He returned to the Cubs for three seasons after 11 years with the Braves.) The Cubs retired 31 in both their honors; they are the only pitchers in franchise history with their number retired.

CONTENDERS

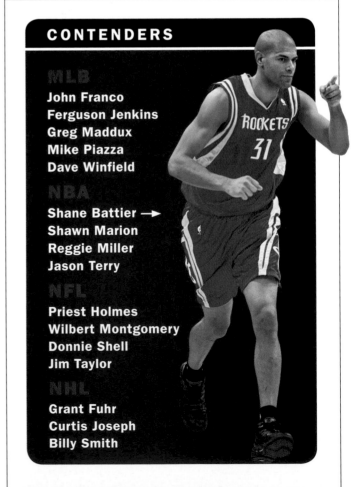

MLB
John Franco
Ferguson Jenkins
Greg Maddux
Mike Piazza
Dave Winfield

NBA
Shane Battier →
Shawn Marion
Reggie Miller
Jason Terry

NFL
Priest Holmes
Wilbert Montgomery
Donnie Shell
Jim Taylor

NHL
Grant Fuhr
Curtis Joseph
Billy Smith

32

TOUGH TO FIND PARKING IN L.A.

Though he wore number 33 at Michigan State, **MAGIC JOHNSON** switched to 32 with the Lakers because Kareem Abdul-Jabbar was already wearing 33.... SHAQUILLE O'NEAL began his career as a 32 with the Magic, but moved up to 34 when he signed with the Lakers because their 32 and 33 had both been retired. Shaq returned to wearing 32 in his next two stops, in Miami and in Phoenix.

THE DEBATE

WHAT DO YOU mean **Sandy Koufax** is third? The same Koufax SPORTS ILLUSTRATED named as its favorite athlete of the 20th century? Yes, Koufax is third, and that tells you less about him than it does about the other iconic figures who have worn number 32.

Koufax is remembered for five electric seasons in which he led the National League in ERA, won three Cy Young Awards and was the ace of a Dodgers team that won two World Series. Also, he refused to pitch in Game 1 of the 1965 World Series because it fell on Yom Kippur, making him a hero to those who prize personal integrity as highly as they do on-field achievement.

But one step up the ladder is **Magic Johnson**, who did it all. He won (an NCAA championship with Michigan State—albeit while wearing a different number—and five NBA titles with the Lakers). He set the NBA assists record (since surpassed by John Stockton). He made dazzling passes worthy of his nickname and, as the smiling avatar of the Showtime Lakers, helped revive the flagging NBA in the 1980s.

But everyone comes second to **Jim Brown**, who embodied greatness. He averaged 104.3 rushing yards a game and won an NFL championship in, of all places, Cleveland. (The Browns haven't won another since that one in 1964.) After nine NFL seasons, at the tender age of 30, he walked away from it all, realizing he'd have more fun as a movie star in Hollywood than as a football player in Ohio. How to measure Brown's star power? Consider that he was the favorite player of Elvis Presley, who would try to walk like Brown in his own football games. When Elvis wants to be you, you're an easy choice at any number.

> ➤ **THE VERDICT**
JIM BROWN

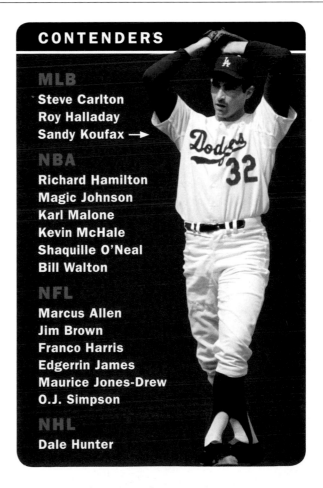

CONTENDERS

MLB
Steve Carlton
Roy Halladay
Sandy Koufax ➤

NBA
Richard Hamilton
Magic Johnson
Karl Malone
Kevin McHale
Shaquille O'Neal
Bill Walton

NFL
Marcus Allen
Jim Brown
Franco Harris
Edgerrin James
Maurice Jones-Drew
O.J. Simpson

NHL
Dale Hunter

33

BETTER NOW THAN LAETTNER

It was out of admiration for Magic Johnson that GRANT HILL wore 32 in high school, but he couldn't take the number at Duke because Christian Laettner was wearing it. Hill learned Magic's college number was 33 and switched to that, and he stuck with it through college and four NBA teams. . . . A huge Babe Ruth fan, pitcher DAVID WELLS asked to wear number 3 with the Yankees. When his request was denied he settled for 33.

CONTENDERS

MLB
Jose Canseco
Eddie Murray
Jason Varitek
Larry Walker
David Wells

NBA
Kareem Abdul-Jabbar
Larry Bird
Patrick Ewing
Grant Hill
Alonzo Mourning
Scottie Pippen

NFL
Sammy Baugh
Tony Dorsett →
Ollie Matson

NHL
Patrick Roy
Henrik Sedin

THE DEBATE

THAT THERE IS even an argument—and a close one—at number 33 says much about the personas of the two top contenders, **Kareem Abdul-Jabbar** and **Larry Bird**.

On achievements alone, this should be no contest. Abdul-Jabbar is the NBA's alltime leading scorer, 1,459 points ahead of Karl Malone and 6,095 ahead of Michael Jordan. He's third in rebounds and in blocked shots. He won six MVP awards with the Bucks and Lakers. His teams won six NBA championships.

But Abdul-Jabbar's chief competitor is in the race—because he was, chiefly, a competitor. Whereas the center could seem aloof, up there alone with his sky-hook, Bird was scrapping every second. He won three league MVP awards and his Celtics took three titles, but what stands out are the moments that earned him the nickname Larry Legend. Whether he was stealing an inbounds pass from Isiah Thomas in the final seconds of a playoff game, or going shot for shot with Dominique Wilkins in a Game 7 showdown, or arriving at the All-Star Game three-point contest and asking, "Which one of you is going to come in second?" the Hick from French Lick embodied what *Hoosiers* represented as a movie: an indomitable spirit. He did this as a college 33 too, carrying a humble Indiana State program to the 1979 NCAA finals.

Of course Jabbar, who also wore number 33 at UCLA, had an amazing college career too, winning three NCAA titles. His record is too much for even Bird to overcome. Of the other contenders, the third slot goes to **Sammy Baugh** *(above)*, a complete football player: In 1943 he led the league in completion percentage, in interceptions on defense, and in punting average. Impressive, but it still doesn't rise to Kareem's heights.

➤ **THE VERDICT**
KAREEM ABDUL-JABBAR

34

THE DEBATE

IN MOST CASES players who split their careers among multiple numbers have weakened cases for the top spot at a particular one. But for **Shaquille O'Neal** a number switch helps (or at least doesn't hurt). It was as a 34 that he was at his best—and even without him the number 33 is crowded with NBA alltime greats.

Shaq wore 32 when he was with the Magic for the first four years of his career, a period in which he seemed more interested in rapping and making terrible movies than he did in chasing rings. He also wore 33 and 36 in his late career ramblings, winning a championship with the former on his back for the Heat in 2006. But it was as number 34 of the Lakers that Shaq dominated the league. He won three championships and was named the MVP of the Finals each time. It was in L.A. that he won his only league MVP award. That run is what slots him ahead of an impressive NBA group at 34 that includes, in order, **Hakeem Olajuwon**, **Paul Pierce** and **Charles Barkley.** (Yes, Pierce over Barkley, even if Sir Charles is the most entertaining studio analyst in any sport.)

But they all take a back seat to **Walter Payton**, who just did everything well. As a Bears rookie in 1975 he ran back kicks and led the NFL in yards per return. Then he became the premier running back in the game and a devastating blocker. He was also more durable than the other great back of his era, **Earl Campbell**, missing just one game in his 12-season career.

When Payton retired he held the NFL records in rushing yards and touchdowns. After he died in 1999 the NFL renamed its Man of the Year award, given for works off the field, for him. Here he's the man of the number.

➤ **THE VERDICT**
WALTER PAYTON

IT WAS 34 OR NOTHING

PAUL PIERCE was given 34 in high school because it was the team's biggest uniform and the only one that fit. . . . NOLAN RYAN's 34 was retired by the Rangers and the Astros, his 30 was retired by the Angels. He is the only player to have his number retired by three teams. . . . Smart dad: the Pirates' DANIEL MCCUTCHEN sold 34 to A.J. BURNETT for a college fund set up in his unborn daughter's name.

CONTENDERS

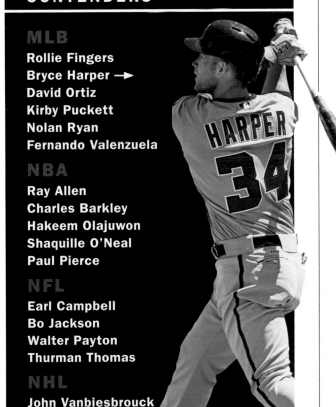

MLB
Rollie Fingers
Bryce Harper ➤
David Ortiz
Kirby Puckett
Nolan Ryan
Fernando Valenzuela

NBA
Ray Allen
Charles Barkley
Hakeem Olajuwon
Shaquille O'Neal
Paul Pierce

NFL
Earl Campbell
Bo Jackson
Walter Payton
Thurman Thomas

NHL
John Vanbiesbrouck

35

PIONEER BETWEEN THE PIPES

The first NHL goalie to wear 35 was TONY ESPOSITO, for the Blackhawks in 1970. He said he "wanted something to make [him] stand out for people to notice." He won three Vezina Trophies wearing the number, which Chicago retired for him in 1988. . . . REGGIE LEWIS, who died at age 27 of heart disease, had his 35 retired by the Celtics and by his college, Northeastern. He is the only Northeastern hoops player to have his number retired.

CONTENDERS

MLB
Rickey Henderson
Mike Mussina
Phil Niekro
Frank Thomas
Justin Verlander →

NBA
Kevin Durant
Darrell Griffith
Reggie Lewis

NFL
Bill Dudley
Calvin Hill
John Henry Johnson
Pete Pihos
Aeneas Williams

NHL
Tony Esposito
Jean-Sebastien Giguere
Mike Richter

THE CHALLENGE at 35 is weighing a full career against a partial. Still in his mid-20s, **Kevin Durant** *(below)* is on a trajectory to be the best to wear the number. With three NBA scoring titles already, he's set an impressive pace. Of course the same could be said of Tigers pitcher **Justin Verlander**. His 2011 season, in which he won both the AL Cy Young Award and the MVP, was the gem of a four-year run from '09 to '12 in which he averaged nearly 20 wins and led the league in strikeouts three times.

Then came 2013, though, when Verlander turned in a respectable but hardly historic performance (13–12, 3.46 ERA). The dip could, in the long run, turn out to be nothing but a blip. All the same, Verlander's '13 results show the danger in projecting forward on any young player's career with absolute certainty.

The résumé of 2014 Hall of Fame inductee **Frank Thomas**, however, is complete. The Big Hurt was a two-time MVP with the White Sox, and his achievements are especially impressive because he is the rare slugger from his era who was never linked in any way to performance enhancing drugs. Thomas did it with power (521 home runs) and patience (he led the league in walks four times), and his career on-base percentage (.419) is the fifth-highest among players who began their careers after World War II. In his 1994 season his OPS was 1.217, which is the 18th best season ever; everyone who did better is either a certified titan (Babe Ruth, Ted Williams, Rogers Hornsby, Lou Gehrig, Jimmie Foxx) or Barry Bonds or Mark McGwire.

The most complicated 35 to consider is **Rickey Henderson**, who wore it for his first six seasons in Oakland and set the modern single-season stolen base record with the number on his back. But he played more games as a 24 (and also wore 39, 22, 14 and 25). Rickey was spectacular as a 35—but Thomas gets credit for standing by his number.

→ **THE VERDICT**
FRANK THOMAS

36

THE DEBATE

THE CONTRAST in personalities of the top two contenders at this number is marked. Both men are Hall of Fame pitchers, but they had very different careers.

On the one hand there is **Robin Roberts**, who was, first and foremost, a horse. In his prime years of 1950 to '56 he won at least 19 games a season, and for five of those years he led the leagues in innings pitched, averaging 327 per year. It is fitting that his greatest win was the '50 pennant clincher against the Brooklyn Dodgers. In that game, making his third start in five days, he went 10 innings and allowed one run.

Roberts beat people without great velocity or a signature breaking pitch. He did it with control and competitiveness. The marks against Roberts are that after his prime seven seasons, his numbers were pedestrian. He wound up with a career record of 286–245 and a 3.41 ERA, and he held the dubious record of most home runs allowed until he was passed in 2010 by Jamie Moyer.

Which leaves us with **Gaylord Perry**. The tall righty is most remembered for his spitball, which once made him seem like a scoundrel, though nowadays a hidden cache of Vaseline seems quaint. Whatever he did, he certainly wasn't the only one doctoring the ball, but no one did it to greater effect. Perry won two Cy Young Awards, in 1972 and '78, and his career totals (314–265, 3.11 ERA) are a clear step up from Roberts's.

The race for third is between two NFL contemporaries, **Jerome Bettis** and **LeRoy Butler**. The Bus, a two-time All-Pro, is certainly more prominent. Butler was a beast, though, and the four-time All-Pro safety invented the Lambeau Leap in 1993. Still, neither is within spitting distance of Perry.

➤ THE VERDICT
GAYLORD PERRY

92

WEARING A HAND-ME-DOWN

JEFF WEAVER **was** wearing number 36 for the Angels in 2006 when the team designated him for assignment and called up his younger brother JERED WEAVER from the minors to take his spot in the rotation. (Awkward, right?) Jeff was soon traded to the Cardinals, and in '07 Jered switched his number from 56 to his brother's 36. Jeff, meanwhile, continued to wear 36 for the Cardinals, Mariners and Dodgers.

CONTENDERS

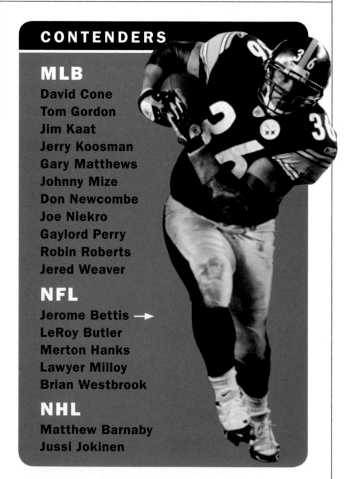

MLB
David Cone
Tom Gordon
Jim Kaat
Jerry Koosman
Gary Matthews
Johnny Mize
Don Newcombe
Joe Niekro
Gaylord Perry
Robin Roberts
Jered Weaver

NFL
Jerome Bettis →
LeRoy Butler
Merton Hanks
Lawyer Milloy
Brian Westbrook

NHL
Matthew Barnaby
Jussi Jokinen

37

THE DEBATE

THE NAME echoes from America's past—you just don't meet a lot of guys named Doak anymore. But **Doak Walker**, football star of the 1940s and '50s, had a game suited for the modern age. He was a swift and shifty halfback, and he knew how to catch the ball.

Despite having won the Heisman at SMU (wearing number 37 there too), plenty of people doubted Walker could make it in the pros because he was only 5' 11" and 173 pounds. He proved them wrong right away. In 1950, Walker's rookie season with the Lions, he had five rushing touchdowns, six receiving touchdowns, kicked 38 extra points and eight field goals, and even intercepted a pass. He was Rookie of the Year and an All-Pro too, the first of four times in his six seasons he would claim that honor. His career averages—4.9 yards a carry, 16.7 yards a reception, 15.8 yards a punt return—paint the portrait of a player whom coaches wanted to get their hands on the ball, any which way. He was a winner too. The six decades of futility Detroit is currently experiencing began shortly after Walker retired. But during his tenure the Lions won two NFL championships. He is in the Hall of Fame, and he's the choice here.

Despite the promise of young pitcher **Stephen Strasburg**, the top three 37s all come from the NFL. **Shaun Alexander** rushed for a league-leading 1,880 yards and 27 touchdowns in 2005. But Alexander really had just three outstanding seasons. Hall of Fame cornerback **Jimmy Johnson** intercepted 47 passes in his 16-year career with the 49ers. If he had offensive stats to match, he might have been more of a challenge to the well-rounded Walker.

→ THE VERDICT

DOAK WALKER

AN EASIER NEGOTIATION

When, after lengthy talks, STEPHEN STRASBURG signed with the Nationals in 2009, he wanted to keep the number he wore at San Diego State. At the time 37 was being worn by third base coach Pat Listach, who surrendered it without any remuneration. . . . In 2003, after joining the Warriors, NICK VAN EXEL switched to 37 from 31 because he had been the 37th pick in the 1993 draft.

CONTENDERS

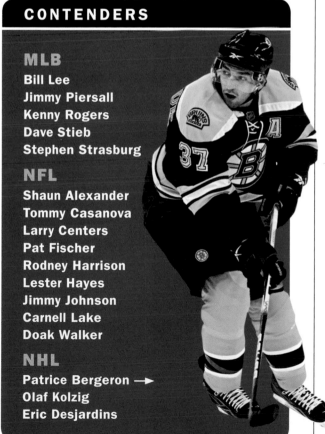

MLB
Bill Lee
Jimmy Piersall
Kenny Rogers
Dave Stieb
Stephen Strasburg

NFL
Shaun Alexander
Tommy Casanova
Larry Centers
Pat Fischer
Rodney Harrison
Lester Hayes
Jimmy Johnson
Carnell Lake
Doak Walker

NHL
Patrice Bergeron →
Olaf Kolzig
Eric Desjardins

38

THE DEBATE

BASEBALL FANS need not have been paying special attention to his uniform to remember that **Curt Schilling** wore number 38. He maintained an entertaining blog called 38pitches and, less happily, he started 38 Studios, a gaming company that went bankrupt in 2012, much to the distress of the state of Rhode Island, which had loaned him $75 million to set up business there.

But the argument in favor of Schilling owning 38 is less for his side ventures than what he did on the mound. He was the ace of a Phillies team that made an unlikely run to the 1993 World Series. Then he and Randy Johnson helped the Diamondbacks break a string of Yankees championships in 2001. Speaking of ending streaks, he helped end the Red Sox' "curse" in '04—in Boston, his Bloody Sock performance at Yankee Stadium in Game 6 of the ALCS ranks in legend a shade below the midnight ride of Paul Revere— and he was an integral part of another World Series win in '07. If there's a quibble, it's that Schilling's career record (216–146, 3.46 ERA) doesn't quite match his aura. But then, he acquired that aura by elevating his performances in the games that mattered most. His postseason numbers are remarkable: 11–2 with a 2.23 ERA. In seven World Series starts, his ERA was even lower, 2.06.

It strengthens Schilling's claim that his strongest competition at 38 is **Arnie Herber**, the Packers quarterback who threw to Don Hutson when the receiver was rewriting NFL pass-catching records in the 1930s and '40s. Herber was one of the first great downfield passers, and for that he is in the Pro Football Hall of Fame. Schilling's history, though, is more enduring.

THE VERDICT
CURT SCHILLING

CLEARED OF THE BEARD

Notably hirsute reliever BRIAN WILSON wore number 38 for six seasons, three All-Star Games and one World Series with the Giants. But after Wilson signed with the rival Dodgers in July 2013, the closer's number didn't have a chance to get cold. It was reissued two months later to highly touted reliever prospect HEATH HEMBREE when he joined San Francisco in September.

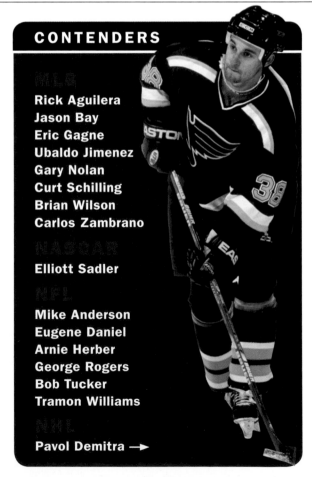

CONTENDERS

MLB

Rick Aguilera
Jason Bay
Eric Gagne
Ubaldo Jimenez
Gary Nolan
Curt Schilling
Brian Wilson
Carlos Zambrano

NASCAR

Elliott Sadler

NFL

Mike Anderson
Eugene Daniel
Arnie Herber
George Rogers
Bob Tucker
Tramon Williams

NHL

Pavol Demitra →

CALLING HIS OWN NUMBER

It was a matter of faith.
As a rookie with the Rams in 2004, STEVEN JACKSON was looking for a number not being worn by any other top running back at the time, and he noticed that 39 was pretty much free. He asked his father for advice and his father independently suggested 39. His father's reasoning was that there are 39 books in the Old Testament. "I said, 'You know what? That's a way to wear my faith on my chest and on my back,'" Jackson once explained.

CONTENDERS

MLB
Len Barker
Roy Campanella
Mike Greenwell
Al Hrabosky
Mike Krukow
Joe Nuxhall
Dave Parker
Mike Witt

NASCAR
Ryan Newman

NFL
Larry Csonka →
Sam Cunningham
Steven Jackson
Hugh McElhenny

NHL
Rick DiPietro
Dominik Hasek
Doug Weight

COMPARING A GOALTENDER and a catcher seems like a reasonable enough proposition, what with the similarities in their equipment, the crouching and the speeding projectiles flying at them. When the two being compared are **Dominik Hasek** (*below*) and **Roy Campanella** the similarities run deeper, as both men were elite at their positions. Hasek won two Hart Trophies as the NHL's most valuable player. Meanwhile, Campanella pulled in three MVP awards in his days with the Dodgers.

The Dominator's feats were great indeed. Though he won the Vezina Trophy six times and twice led the Red Wings to Stanley Cup championships, his most legendary performance came for his native Czech Republic in the 1998 Winter Olympics. The semifinals came down to a shootout, and he was perfect against Canada's battery of future Hall of Famers. Then in the gold medal game he shut out Russia to give the Czechs an improbable gold medal.

Campanella's triumphs encompass more than just on-field excellence. He spent the first eight years of his career playing in the Negro and Mexican leagues, only joining the Dodgers in 1948 at age 26, as the sixth African-American in Major League Baseball. With a rifle arm and a great store of power in his short, squat frame, Campanella helped his Dodgers to five World Series, meeting frustration at the hands of the Yankees in all but one. Then at age 36, with a few good years still in front of him, he was in a car wreck that left him paralyzed from the shoulders down. It was as a paraplegic that Campanella may have made his greatest impression. He dealt with his setback with rare good cheer, enduring grueling therapy to regain some use of his arms, working for the Dodgers in scouting and community relations, and even coaching at spring training in Dodgertown, until his death in 1993.

In a contest between two greats, it's the memory of Campanella's courage that gives him the edge.

→ THE VERDICT

ROY CAMPANELLA

NHL
BY THE NUMBERS

What sweater has the richest history at each position? If you were to build a team by numbers, these are the digits you'd want to draft at each spot

RIGHT WING 9

Glenn Anderson, Andy Bathgate, Gordie Howe, Lanny McDonald, Maurice Richard
Next best: 22 (Mike Bossy, Dino Ciccarelli, Mike Gartner)

CENTER 19

Rick MacLeish, Jean Ratelle, Joe Sakic, Joe Thornton, Bryan Trottier, Steve Yzerman
Next best: 16 (Bobby Clarke, Marcel Dionne, Henri Richard)

LEFT WING 9

John Bucyk, Dick Duff, Clark Gillies, Bobby Hull, Paul Kariya
Next best: 7 (Bill Barber, Ted Lindsay, Keith Tkachuk)

DEFENSEMAN 4

Bill Gadsby, Ron Greschner, Red Kelly, Kevin Lowe, Bobby Orr, Scott Stevens
Next best: 2 (Doug Harvey, Brian Leetch, Al MacInnis)

GOALIE 1

Johnny Bower, Ed Giacomin, Glenn Hall, Bernie Parent, Jacques Plante, Terry Sawchuk
Next best: 30 (Ed Belfour, Martin Brodeur, Parent)

21

It has adorned 455 different sweaters

0, 98

One each: Neil Sheehy (0) and Brian Lawton (98)

9

10 trophies, led by Mr. Hockey's six

19

Six: Richards, Robinson, Sakic, Toews, Trottier, Yzerman

9

It has been hung in the rafters by 11 teams

Steve Yzerman

40

THE DEBATE

THIS NUMBER is, in a sports context, most commonly associated with speed. *What's his time in the 40?* It's a happy coincidence that the top two players to wear this jersey were known for their jets.

Our top pick is **Gale Sayers**, who scored 22 touchdowns as a Bears rookie in 1965 and was All-Pro for five years before knee injuries cut short his career. But what an impression that brief career made. Former NFL coach Mike Shanahan, who only witnessed Sayers as a fan, once described Sayers's elusiveness to SI as being, "like defenders were trying to catch smoke in air." Dick LeBeau, the great defensive coordinator who also played against Sayers, recalled, "He always had another gear. He would be even better today, with spread offenses and hash marks in the middle of the field." It's the breathlessness of his admirers that makes Sayers the choice. Also, two words: *Brian's Song*.

The next speedster down from Sayers is **Elroy (Crazy Legs) Hirsch**. A master at getting behind defenses, the Hall of Fame Rams receiver had three full seasons in which he averaged more than 20 yards per catch—and this was in the 1950s, when offenses were mostly built around the run. In '51, in a 12-game season, he caught 17 touchdowns and set a league record for receiving yards with 1,495. The mark stood for a decade.

In the NBA the number 40 has been worn by some memorable frontcourt players. There's **Bill Laimbeer**, who won two titles as a Bad Boy Piston, and Heat three-time champ **Udonis Haslem**. The pick of the group, though, is **Shawn Kemp**, who starred on a 64-win Sonics team that had the bad fortune of meeting Michael Jordan's 72-win Bulls team in the 1996 Finals.

→ **THE VERDICT**
GALE SAYERS

A SOLDIER'S NUMBER

PAT TILLMAN made the rare choice to leave the Arizona Cardinals, where he had been a starting safety, and enlist in the U.S. Army to become a Ranger. He was killed in Afghanistan in 2004. One of the many tributes he inspired: When MIKE RICCI left the NHL's Sharks for the Coyotes the center switched to number 40 to honor Tillman. The two had met a few times in San Jose, Tillman's hometown.

CONTENDERS

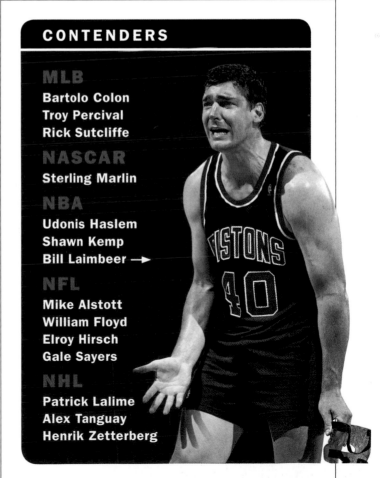

MLB
Bartolo Colon
Troy Percival
Rick Sutcliffe

NASCAR
Sterling Marlin

NBA
Udonis Haslem
Shawn Kemp
Bill Laimbeer →

NFL
Mike Alstott
William Floyd
Elroy Hirsch
Gale Sayers

NHL
Patrick Lalime
Alex Tanguay
Henrik Zetterberg

41

NOT THE RETIRING TYPES

TOM SEAVER **is the only** Mets player to have his number retired, although the team has bestowed the honor on two managers, GIL HODGES (14) and CASEY STENGEL (37). . . . When he joined the Mavericks in 1998, DIRK NOWITZKI wanted 14, which had been his number as a pro baller in his native Germany. But that was taken by Robert Pack, so Nowitzki flipped the digits. He wore 14 when he played for the German national team.

CONTENDERS

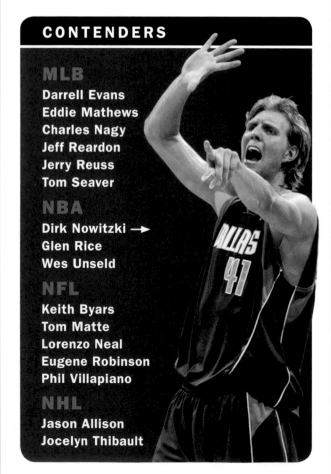

MLB
Darrell Evans
Eddie Mathews
Charles Nagy
Jeff Reardon
Jerry Reuss
Tom Seaver

NBA
Dirk Nowitzki →
Glen Rice
Wes Unseld

NFL
Keith Byars
Tom Matte
Lorenzo Neal
Eugene Robinson
Phil Villapiano

NHL
Jason Allison
Jocelyn Thibault

IF YOU WERE your team's Opening Day starter 16 times in your career, you were on top of your game for a long time. That was certainly true of **Tom Seaver**. As the 24-year-old clubhouse leader of the 1969 Miracle Mets, the righthander kept a young team rolling all the way to an improbable World Series. (It's hard to lose momentum when your ace goes 25–7.) Now flip forward to Seaver at age 36, when his fastball didn't trip the radar gun as it once did and he was striking out half as many batters per nine innings as he did in his prime: Seaver still went 14–2 and nearly won his fourth Cy Young Award. His résumé includes 311 wins and 3,640 strikeouts.

Seaver's closest challenger for supremacy at number 41, **Eddie Mathews** (*right*), hit 512 home runs and is on the short list for greatest third baseman ever. But Seaver is on the same list for right-handed pitchers—a tougher list to make.

The most intriguing comparison at number 41 is between **Wes Unseld** and **Dirk Nowitzki**, who provide a pure contrast in basketball styles. Unseld, despite being 6' 7", was one of the NBA's top centers thanks to his mastery of the game's nuances. His game was about rebounding (14.0 career average), picks and defense more than it was scoring (10.8 career average). Then there's Nowitzki, who has a center's height (7 feet) but plays forward and devastates defenses with a feathery jump shot. The standard joke about Nowitzki early in his career was that his first name should be Irk, because he had no D—but he developed into a decent defender. The greatest point on Nowitzki's behalf is that he was the main man on the Mavericks team that took down LeBron James's Miami Heat for the 2011 NBA title. Unseld's championship came in 1978, during a down period in the NBA before Larry Bird and Magic Johnson reinvigorated the league. In number 41's second division, Nowitzki earns the nod.

→ THE VERDICT
TOM SEAVER

42

THE DEBATE

HE IS THE most important athlete in American history, the man who broke the color barrier in baseball in 1947, seven years before the Supreme Court ruled in *Brown* v. *Board of Education* that school segregation laws were unconstitutional. He changed not only sports, but also the country. Beyond that, he was a heck of an athlete, a four-sport star at UCLA who then overcame threats and taunts that would unnerve most men to become one of the greatest second basemen ever. He was a career .311 hitter for the Brooklyn Dodgers, the 1949 NL MVP and a terror on the bases. In 1997, 50 years after his major league debut, Major League Baseball retired 42 leaguewide in his honor. If any player owns any number, **Jackie Robinson** owns 42. All others who wore the number are vying for second. That contest is an interesting one, though, because number 42 also features baseball's greatest closer, **Mariano Rivera**, and football's ultimate defensive back, **Ronnie Lott**.

Rivera, baseball's alltime saves leader, had 11 seasons with an ERA of 1.94 or less. He played on five World Series winners, four as the closer. He was a security blanket for that Yankees dynasty. But Lott did some winning too. San Francisco won four Super Bowls with Lott patrolling the defensive backfield. If Rivera's presence reassured the Yankees, Lott's fired up the 49ers, demanding more of teammates even in the best of times. Before the 1986 season the injured Lott had a choice: Remove part of his pinkie and miss three weeks, or undergo surgery, insert a pin and miss eight weeks. He told the doctors to take off the pinkie—just the type of dedication and competitive spirit with which Robinson had imbued 42 decades before.

➤ THE VERDICT

JACKIE ROBINSON

LIFE AFTER RETIREMENT

Thirteen players were grandfathered into the use of 42 after it was retired for JACKIE ROBINSON in 1997. The last to wear it regularly was MARIANO RIVERA, who retired in 2013. . . . MO VAUGHN was the last to wear 42 for three teams (Red Sox, Mets and Angels). . . . In 2007 KEN GRIFFEY JR. asked to wear 42 for the annual Jackie Robinson Day; today all players and coaches are invited to wear the number to support the occasion.

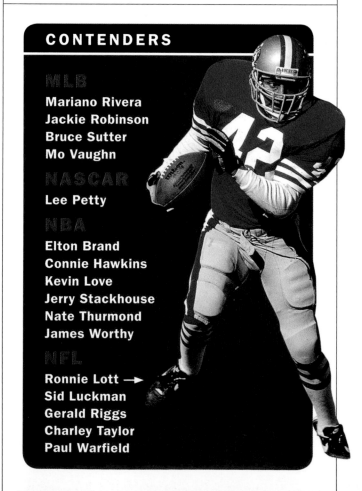

CONTENDERS

MLB
Mariano Rivera
Jackie Robinson
Bruce Sutter
Mo Vaughn

NASCAR
Lee Petty

NBA
Elton Brand
Connie Hawkins
Kevin Love
Jerry Stackhouse
Nate Thurmond
James Worthy

NFL
Ronnie Lott ➤
Sid Luckman
Gerald Riggs
Charley Taylor
Paul Warfield

43

THE DEBATE

IN JUDGING the best 43s, it's tempting to skip past their accomplishments and go straight to their appearances. Because they all have a look. **Richard Petty** has those shades and that hat. **Troy Polamalu** has locks so flowing he does shampoo commercials. Then there's **Dennis Eckersley**, whose mustache and middle-parted shoulder-length hair is definitely a style, even if no one is quite sure what to call it.

Just by looks, the choice would be Petty because, unlike hair-dependent styles, hats-and-shades ages well. On performance Petty is the choice, too. He is a seven-time NASCAR champion and his 200 race wins are a record, that will stand for a long time (the closest active driver, Jeff Gordon, has 88 victories). Petty is the King indeed.

One curiosity about the number 43 is that no Pro Football Hall of Famer has worn it, not even briefly. That will surely change about five years after Polamalu pulls off his helmet for the last time. An ideal safety, he is a savage hitter with the ability to make plays in the Steelers' defensive backfield or deep in coverage. He is also brilliant at disguising his intentions, so quarterbacks never know where he will pop up.

Our third man, Eckersley, is a bridge between baseball eras. He began his career as a very good starting pitcher, throwing a no-hitter in 1977 and going 20–8 in '78. But he truly blossomed when he moved to the bullpen. In '89 he was the closer for the World Series champion A's, and in '92 he won the Cy Young Award and the AL MVP award, with a 7–1 record, 51 saves and a 1.91 ERA. Among closers, Eck was king of the hill until Mariano Rivera came along. But at number 43 he's no match for the King.

➤ THE VERDICT

RICHARD PETTY

THE KING OF CLEVELAND

Casual observers were surprised when NBA center BRAD DAUGHERTY transitioned from the court to the track to become a race car owner and TV analyst. But those who knew the story of his uniform number might have seen this move coming. The five-time All-Star wore 43 during his eight seasons with the Cavaliers as a tribute to his father's favorite driver, RICHARD PETTY.

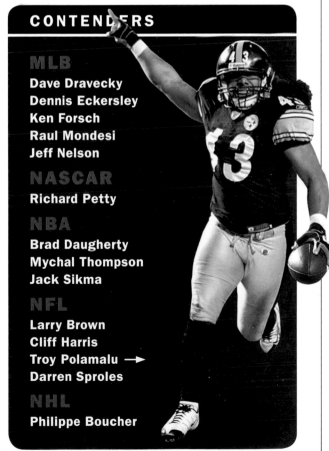

CONTENDERS

MLB
Dave Dravecky
Dennis Eckersley
Ken Forsch
Raul Mondesi
Jeff Nelson

NASCAR
Richard Petty

NBA
Brad Daugherty
Mychal Thompson
Jack Sikma

NFL
Larry Brown
Cliff Harris
Troy Polamalu ➤
Darren Sproles

NHL
Philippe Boucher

THE DEBATE

ONE MAN STOOD on the mound, wearing number 44 on his uniform. Another 44 stood at the plate, awaiting his pitch—which came, a high fastball down the middle. The batter lined it over the wall in left centerfield, and the two 44s were forever linked. True, **Al Downing**'s place in history is as a footnote, as the pitcher who gave up the home run that broke Babe Ruth's mark of 714, while **Hank Aaron** endures as the former—and to some, the still reigning and legitimate—Home Run King. However you sort out the nomenclature, of this there is no doubt: Aaron's 23-year career was astounding. In addition to his 755 home runs, he still holds the major league records for total bases, extra-base hits and RBIs, and his 3,771 hits place him third behind Pete Rose and Ty Cobb.

Aaron achieved his marks with a steadiness and consistency that informs the nickname Hammerin' Hank, and separates him from more flamboyant 44s such as **Reggie Jackson**, who wore the number in his Yankees and Angels years. Some dazzling scorers wore 44 in the NBA (**George Gervin**, **Pete Maravich**) but the strong second at this number is another tenacious athlete, **Jerry West**. He was the sort to play through a broken nose, and he made so many game-winning shots that he was nicknamed Mr. Clutch. The guard's career averages (27.0 points, 5.8 rebounds, 6.7 assists) speak to the completeness of his game. His Lakers made the Finals in nine of his 14 seasons, though they often fell short there against Bill Russell's Celtics. (West was the MVP of the 1969 Finals, the only time the honor has gone to a player on the losing team). In this debate, West is in a familiar spot: he finishes second to a legend.

→ THE VERDICT

HANK AARON

CALLING ALL ORANGEMEN

The number 44 is valued no place more than at Syracuse. The digits were retired in 2005 in honor of the greats who wore it there, a list that includes JIM BROWN, ERNIE DAVIS, and FLOYD LITTLE in football and DERRICK COLEMAN in basketball. Beyond that, the school's zip code was changed from 13210 to 13244, and all the numbers in the university's phone system now begin with a 44.

CONTENDERS

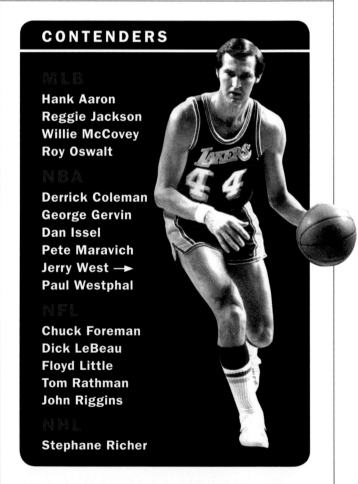

MLB

Hank Aaron
Reggie Jackson
Willie McCovey
Roy Oswalt

NBA

Derrick Coleman
George Gervin
Dan Issel
Pete Maravich
Jerry West →
Paul Westphal

NFL

Chuck Foreman
Dick LeBeau
Floyd Little
Tom Rathman
John Riggins

NHL

Stephane Richer

45

IF HE COULD BE LIKE MIKE

He is remembered as a 23, but MICHAEL JORDAN briefly wore 45 upon his return from his first retirement, with 17 games to go in the 1994–95 season. He switched back to 23 after losing a playoff game to Orlando in which Magic guard Nick Anderson declared "Number 45 is not number 23." Jordan said the change helped his confidence: "Twenty-three is me." Jordan had worn 45 during his baseball experiment with the Birmingham Barons.

CONTENDERS

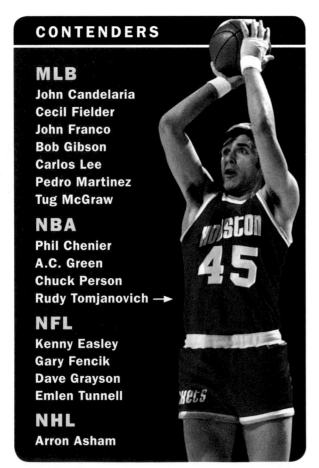

MLB
John Candelaria
Cecil Fielder
John Franco
Bob Gibson
Carlos Lee
Pedro Martinez
Tug McGraw

NBA
Phil Chenier
A.C. Green
Chuck Person
Rudy Tomjanovich →

NFL
Kenny Easley
Gary Fencik
Dave Grayson
Emlen Tunnell

NHL
Arron Asham

IT'S AN OLD-FASHIONED pitching duel, and it's a doozy: **Bob Gibson** vs. **Pedro Martinez**.

The matchup provides an amusing contrast in personalities. Off the mound at least, Martinez, a slim, 5' 11" Dominican native, had an endearingly goofy side. The 6' 1" Gibson (*below*), however, lived to intimidate. "You wouldn't see him talk to the other players at all," recalled former Cardinals manager Red Schoendienst in a 1993 SI story. "It seemed like he just hated them. He said. 'I ain't going to get friendly with anybody.' " Former Tigers pitcher Denny McLain also testified to Gibson's unremitting surliness.

"We did the Bob Hope show together [in 1968] and the [bleepin'] guy barely spoke to me." Gibson certainly carried himself like a pitcher second to no one.

But examine the numbers and another picture emerges. One might expect that a turn to metrics would help Gibson, as the Cardinals righthander put together arguably the most statistically impressive pitching season of the modern era: In 1968 he threw 13 shutouts on the way to a 1.12 ERA. That's the best single-season ERA by a pitcher since Dutch Leonard's 0.96 in 1914. But the mark needs some context, for 1968 is known as the Year of the Pitcher. That season seven pitchers had ERAs below 2.00, and the NL batting average was just .243.

By contrast, the five seasons in which Martinez led the majors in ERA came during a time in which hitters where asserting their dominion through means fair and unfair. It was a time of artificially enhanced muscles, and home run totals grew in concert. Not only were the leaguewide batting averages notably higher in Martinez's day, but the home run rate was double compared to 1968. Despite this offensive surge, Pedro's career ERA is the merest shade behind Gibson's (2.93 to 2.91). Also, if we're counting dominant seasons, Martinez has three Cy Youngs to Gibson's two. The true ace here is Pedro.

→ THE VERDICT

PEDRO MARTINEZ

46

THE DEBATE

IT MIGHT SEEM odd to talk about **Andy Pettitte** coming out on top of any broad-survey list, since the pitcher was rarely the most dominant figure on his own staff. This was especially true toward the middle and later parts of his tenure with the Yankees, when he was overshadowed by high-profile hires such as Roger Clemens and CC Sabathia, not to mention Mariano Rivera in the bullpen. But Pettitte was a mighty mound presence when New York was racking up titles in the late 1990s, and he remained consistently good for a long time. From '95 to 2013, Pettitte did not have a losing season, and he started on five World Series winners.

Pettitte stood an imposing 6' 5", as did his closest competitor from the ranks of baseball, **Lee Smith**. The fireballer led the league in saves on four occasions and is third on the alltime list in that category. Still, he's been on the Hall of Fame ballot 12 times without earning enshrinement. There's just something about Smith—who played for eight teams and only pitched in two playoffs series in 18 seasons, both times for teams that lost—which prevents a sense of greatness from coalescing around him.

Ranking ahead of Smith at this number is Raiders tight end **Todd Christensen**, who led the NFL in receptions in 1983 and '86, and had three 1,000-yard seasons. But he had a relatively brief window of excellence. He came into the league as a fullback and initially resisted the change to tight end. Between that and injury, the five-time Pro Bowl performer didn't emerge as an offensive weapon until his fifth year. He then had four good-to-great seasons and was pretty much done. That hardly compares with Pettitte's long run.

➤ THE VERDICT
ANDY PETTITTE

SHOW ME THE ORIGINAL

While he isn't the greatest 46, no player is more associated with the number than Bears safety DOUG PLANK. Defensive coordinator Buddy Ryan used Plank's number to name his 46 defense in the 1980s. . . . TIM MCDONALD, a six-time Pro Bowl safety for the Cardinals and 49ers, made the best pop-culture contribution by a 46, inspiring the line "show me the money" in *Jerry Maguire.*

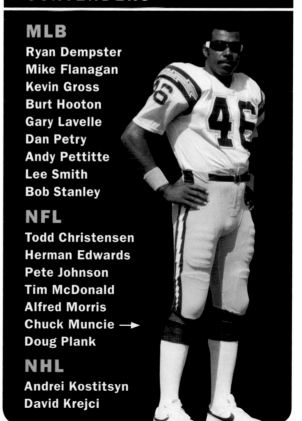

CONTENDERS

MLB
Ryan Dempster
Mike Flanagan
Kevin Gross
Burt Hooton
Gary Lavelle
Dan Petry
Andy Pettitte
Lee Smith
Bob Stanley

NFL
Todd Christensen
Herman Edwards
Pete Johnson
Tim McDonald
Alfred Morris
Chuck Muncie ➤
Doug Plank

NHL
Andrei Kostitsyn
David Krejci

47

SHOULD BE AUTOMATIC

Only one NBA starter has ever worn 47 as his main number, and it is a pun so obvious he should have thought of it first. If you are from Russia and your initials are AK (and you aren't sensitive to being associated with an automatic weapon, even in a lighthearted way), you should be wearing 47. This was pointed out to ANDREI KIRILENKO by teammate Quincy Lewis, a little-used swingman who in four seasons had 96 career assists (97 if you count that one).

CONTENDERS

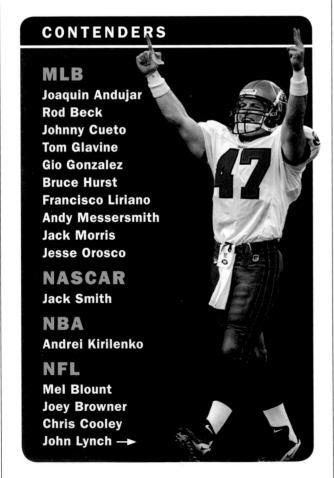

MLB
Joaquin Andujar
Rod Beck
Johnny Cueto
Tom Glavine
Gio Gonzalez
Bruce Hurst
Francisco Liriano
Andy Messersmith
Jack Morris
Jesse Orosco

NASCAR
Jack Smith

NBA
Andrei Kirilenko

NFL
Mel Blount
Joey Browner
Chris Cooley
John Lynch →

THE GREATNESS among those who have worn 47 is concentrated in two sports (baseball and football) and largely two positions (pitcher and defensive back). The argument comes down to two men, **Mel Blount** and **Tom Glavine**.

Blount is clearly at the head of the class of defensive backs, even with competition from **John Lynch**, a nine-time Pro Bowler with Tampa Bay and Denver from 1993 to 2007, and a Super Bowl winner in '02. As great as Lynch was over a long period of time, he is overshadowed by Blount. The Pittsburgh cornerback stood 6' 3"

and weighed 205 pounds, and he was the leader of the backfield on the vaunted Steel Curtain defense, which won four Super Bowls. But more than that, Blount was so good that he forced a change in the rules of the game. Blount so physically dominated the receivers of his day that in 1978 the NFL rewrote its rule book to ban defensive backs from making contact with receivers more than five yards from the line of scrimmage. Blount continued to dominate anyway: Three of his Pro Bowl appearances and one of his two All-Pro selections came after the new rules were in place.

Like Blount, Glavine (*above*) was part of a great unit—the Braves' rotation of the 1990s. While those Atlanta teams are remembered mostly for falling short of the big prize, it was Glavine who came up big when those Braves won their one World Series, against the Indians in '95. In the clinching Game Six the lefthander pitched eight innings of one-hit, shutout ball, allowing only a bloop single to a strong-hitting Cleveland team. It's the gem of an outstanding career that includes 305 wins and two Cy Young Awards

Glavine and Blount are the only two Hall of Famers to wear 47 for the duration of their careers. Between them it's Blount who gets the nod—as good as the Brave was, it's the Steeler who so overwhelmed his opponents that it seemed unfair.

➤ THE VERDICT
MEL BLOUNT

48

THE DEBATE

ONLY ONE ATHLETE who has worn number 48 stands out as a titan of his sport, and he's a man who's not yet done building his legend: **Jimmie Johnson**. He won five consecutive NASCAR championships from 2006 through '10, the only driver in history with such a run, and 14 years into his career his win total is already in the alltime Top 10 list, with plenty of driving ahead of him. If there's one area in which Johnson falls short it's the myth department—he's all focus and analysis, a clinical champion in a daredevil sport. And he's one of the sport's good guys, which doesn't always make for electric copy. But he is indisputably one of NASCAR's greatest drivers ever.

A strong challenger to Johnson is **Sam McDowell**, a Cleveland pitcher with a fastball so fearsome that an SI coverline from the 1966 season posed the question FASTER THAN KOUFAX? It is in strikeouts that McDowell's record holds up best. He led the majors in Ks per nine innings five times, and his career number (8.86) is 13th alltime, ahead of such figures as Roger Clemens and Mariano Rivera. But a broader review certainly tamps down the enthusiasm. For instance, Sudden Sam's career record is a mere 141–134, he never pitched in a World Series, and his career ERA (3.17) was just better than average.

Football's lone Hall of Famer to wear this number is **Les Richter**, a Rams linebacker who was named to eight consecutive Pro Bowls beginning in 1954. The most interesting detail about Richter is that the Rams traded 11 players for his draft rights, thus setting the stage for future pick-laden deals involving Herschel Walker and Ricky Williams—except this one actually worked out.

➤ THE VERDICT

JIMMIE JOHNSON

HAIL TO THE CHIEF

Michigan retired former President GERALD FORD's number 48 in 1994 but brought it back into circulation in 2012, along with two other retired numbers (Bennie Oosterbaan's 47 and Ron Kramer's 87). Now any new 48 wears a commemorative patch in honor of Ford, who played center and linebacker and was voted the Wolverines' most valuable player for the 1934 season.

CONTENDERS

MLB
Mark Davis
Ralph Garr
Travis Hafner
Torii Hunter
Ramon Martinez
Sam McDowell
Andy Pafko
Paul Quantrill
Rick Reuschel

NASCAR
Jimmie Johnson

NFL
Stephen Davis
Ken Ellis
Wes Hopkins
Daryl Johnston ➤
Les Richter

NHL
Daniel Briere

49

THE DEBATE

TWO PLAYERS are in their sport's Hall of Fame, and a third isn't. So it should be simple: One of the guys with the bust wins, right? Number 49 features the NFL's **Bobby Mitchell** who is enshrined in Canton and baseball's **Hoyt Wilhelm** who has a plaque in Cooperstown. But there's a case to be made for an unenshrined man, **Ron Guidry**.

The argument begins with Guidry's 1978 season. The skinny Yankees lefthander's record was an astounding 25–3, with a 1.74 ERA and nine shutouts. And Louisiana Lightning delivered when it mattered most—he was the starter in the Yankees–Red Sox one-game tie-breaker memorable for Bucky Dent's home run, then he went on to win both his postseason starts, allowing two runs in 17 innings as the Yankees won the World Series. Overall his postseason record was 5-2, and he had a career record of 170–91 with a 3.29 ERA. It's likely a lack of longevity that keeps Guidry out of Cooperstown—his body of work includes only 10 seasons of at least 20 starts—but his pace would be the envy of many pitchers in the Hall. Wilhelm is a tough comparison because the knuckleballer usually worked in relief, and his 2.52 ERA is better than Guidry's. But Guidry was the star that shone brighter.

As for Mitchell, he was a speedy waterbug who split his time between running back, wide receiver and kick returner for the Browns and Redskins. His most statistically impressive seasons came for Washington in 1962 and '63, when he led the NFL in receiving yards with 1,384 and 1,436. The trouble with Mitchell is that his best years, in Washington, were given in the service of forgettable losing teams, while Guidry's heroics were the kind that made baseball history.

➤ THE VERDICT
RON GUIDRY

YOU'RE IN THE NO-SPIN ZONE

It's almost like a secret society. Beginning with HOYT WILHELM in the 1950s, many knuckleballers have worn number 49 as a sign of fraternity—including CHARLIE HOUGH, TOM CANDIOTTI and TIM WAKEFIELD. Hough tutored Wakefield in the art of the pitch. . . . In addition to knuckleballers, 49 was also worn by one noted knucklehead: loudmouth Braves pitcher JOHN ROCKER.

CONTENDERS

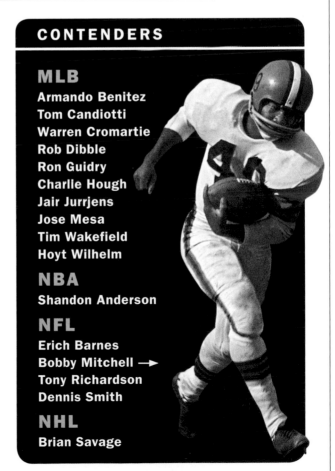

MLB
Armando Benitez
Tom Candiotti
Warren Cromartie
Rob Dibble
Ron Guidry
Charlie Hough
Jair Jurrjens
Jose Mesa
Tim Wakefield
Hoyt Wilhelm

NBA
Shandon Anderson

NFL
Erich Barnes
Bobby Mitchell ➔
Tony Richardson
Dennis Smith

NHL
Brian Savage

BIG MEN ON CAMPUS

BY THE NUMBERS

Sometimes a number chooses a player—especially at schools where certain digits are reserved for those deemed worthy of comparison to previous stars at their position

ALABAMA QUARTERBACK 12

Joe Namath (left) and Ken Stabler (right) wore 12 in the 1960s, as did Brodie Croyle and Greg McElroy in the 2000s.

MICHIGAN WIDE RECEIVER 1

Anthony Carter (left), Braylon Edwards (right) and Derrick Alexander made this the mark of the Wolverines' best hands.

NOTRE DAME QUARTERBACK 3

The stars on this list include Joe Montana (left), Rick Mirer (right), George Izo, Daryle Lamonica and Coley O'Brien.

USC LINEBACKER 55

Junior Seau (left), Willie McGinest (right), Chris Claiborne and Keith Rivers parlayed two 5s into top 10 draft spots.

SYRACUSE RUNNING BACK 44

After the rushing heroics of Jim Brown, Ernie Davis and Floyd Little (top to bottom), the Orange retired their number.

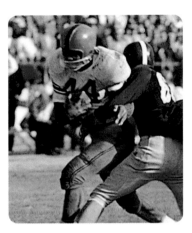

50

THE DEBATE

WERE THE SCOPE of this book restricted to the college ranks, the choice would come down to basketball players: **Rebecca Lobo**, **Tyler Hansbrough** and **Ralph Sampson**. Lobo was a player of the year, a champion, and a breakout star for the women's game. Hansbrough, another player of the year, was also a champion. The most decorated among them was the 7' 4" Sampson, a three-time player of the year at Virginia and a good pro in Houston before injuries cut short his career (rough draft of Yao Ming?).

But the debate here revolves around two 50s who succeeded greatly at the pro level: **David Robinson** and **Mike Singletary**. Singletary, the ferocious Bears middle linebacker, had Hansbrough-like intensity in his gaze. But Singletary was more than just a mad dervish of energy; he was the quarterback for Buddy Ryan's 46 defense. Singletary was named NFL Defensive Player of the Year twice. In 1985, the Bears' Super Bowl season, he led a unit that held opponents to 10 points or less in 11 of 16 regular season games.

Robinson, by contrast, is a Naval Academy graduate who approached competition not with psycho eyes, but with a smile. He was an officer and a gentleman, and he turned the Spurs into winners the moment he arrived in San Antonio. He was NBA Defensive Player of the Year in his third season and MVP in his sixth.

But the Admiral didn't win a championship until Tim Duncan joined him in the frontcourt. The issue is, Robinson left doubt. The year he won MVP, he was destroyed in the playoffs by rival Hakeem Olajuwon. And those titles—were they more about Duncan? With Singletary, there is no doubt.

➤ THE VERDICT

MIKE SINGLETARY

CAN I GET A LEI WITH THAT?

Several athletes from Hawaii have honored their 50th-state heritage with their uniform number, including baseball's **SID FERNANDEZ** and **BENNY AGBAYANI**.... **JAMIE MOYER**, who pitched 25 major league seasons, was a model of endurance, going until age 49, in 2012. But if he had lasted one more season, his age and uniform number would have matched.

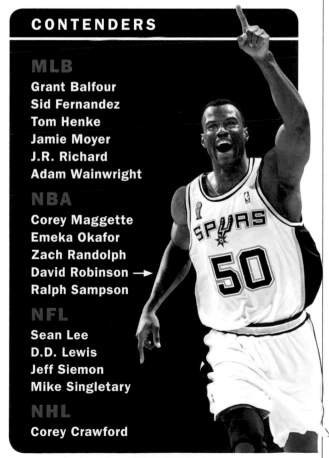

CONTENDERS

MLB
Grant Balfour
Sid Fernandez
Tom Henke
Jamie Moyer
J.R. Richard
Adam Wainwright

NBA
Corey Maggette
Emeka Okafor
Zach Randolph
David Robinson ➤
Ralph Sampson

NFL
Sean Lee
D.D. Lewis
Jeff Siemon
Mike Singletary

NHL
Corey Crawford

51

THE DEBATE

IMAGINE THAT you are standing at the plate, 60 feet, six inches from **Randy Johnson**. He is 6' 10", sporting an unruly mullet, and he is the nastiest strikeout artist in the history of the game—if you don't believe it, check out his whiff rate of 10.6 per nine innings, the highest ever. He peers at you from behind his glove, about to throw a hard projectile at you. Are you intimidated?

Wait a minute, what if you are not you? What if you are . . . **Dick Butkus**? Baseball was not his game, but so what? Competing was.

The depth of talent at number 51 is quite impressive, especially in baseball. There's **Ichiro Suzuki**, who, including his time in Japan, has more than 4,000 hits. Also in the group is **Trevor Hoffman**, the first reliever to save 600 games. But the tops in baseball is Johnson. In addition to his strikeout totals—he led the majors nine times—he also won five Cy Young Awards, including four in a row from 1999 to 2002, and has 303 career victories.

But the winner here is Butkus, because he so completely embodies an archetype—of a middle linebacker, definitely, but also of a defensive football player. Butkus ran amok on the field with a barely controlled aggression. An SI cover in 1970 proclaimed him "the most feared man in the game." While his teams had mixed success, much of this can be ascribed to the great Chicago tradition of middling-to-poor quarterback play. But when, in '70, SI asked NFL coaches to name one player they would choose to start a team with, Butkus was the clear favorite. Not a passer, not a running back, but Butkus. Perhaps it was this: If he was on their team, then they wouldn't have to face him.

➤ **THE VERDICT**
DICK BUTKUS

CONTENDERS

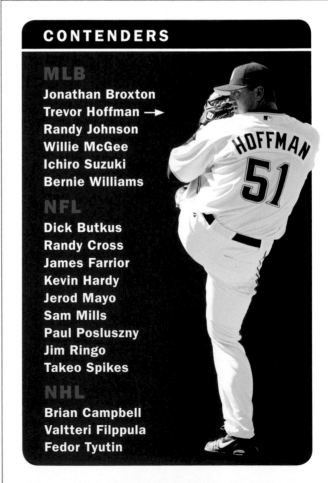

MLB

Jonathan Broxton
Trevor Hoffman ➤
Randy Johnson
Willie McGee
Ichiro Suzuki
Bernie Williams

NFL

Dick Butkus
Randy Cross
James Farrior
Kevin Hardy
Jerod Mayo
Sam Mills
Paul Posluszny
Jim Ringo
Takeo Spikes

NHL

Brian Campbell
Valtteri Filppula
Fedor Tyutin

52

NOT EXACTLY A BLAZER OF GLORY

During his one year at Ohio State, GREG ODEN wore number 20. But he had to switch to 52 as a pro because the Trail Blazers had retired 20 for Maurice Lucas. After playing in only 82 games in five seasons because of knee injuries, Oden dumped 52 and reverted to 20 when he signed with the Heat in 2013. . . . Linebacker PATRICK WILLIS was offered a choice of four numbers with the 49ers and chose 52 in part because, as he explained, "[even numbers] seem more smooth."

CONTENDERS

MLB
Mike Boddicker
Jose Contreras
CC Sabathia

NBA
Matt Geiger
Brad Miller
Jamaal Wilkes
Buck Williams

NFL
Robert Brazile
Frank Gatski
Ted Johnson
Ray Lewis
Clay Matthews →
Mike Webster
Patrick Willis

NHL
Adam Foote
Mike Green

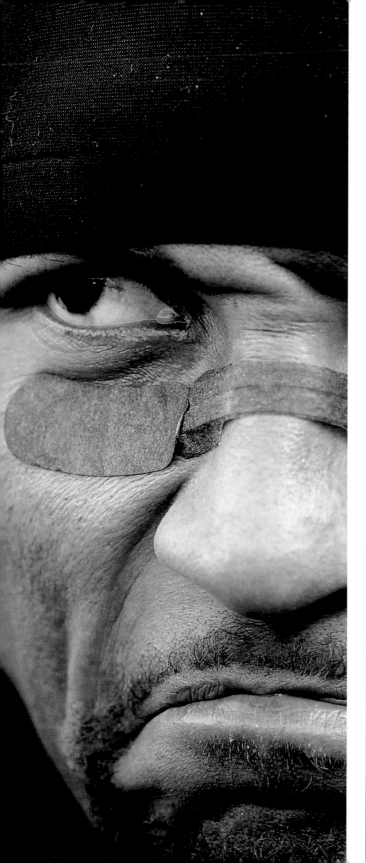

THE DEBATE

THE TWO GREATEST athletes to wear number 52 are football players with very different personalities. Consider **Mike Webster**, the Steelers center who made the NFL's All-Decade teams for the 1970s and '80s. The man was a model of humility. Iron Mike (*below*) died in 2002, at age 50, after playing in more games (220) than any other Steeler. He suffered from brain damage attributed to his playing career, one in which he missed just four games over his first 16 seasons. At the time of Webster's death SI's Paul Zimmerman recalled that when it came to being interviewed, Webster was insightful and deferential. Whenever the two were done talking, Webster would point toward Bradshaw or Lynn Swann or Joe Greene and say, "Better go talk to the superstars."

Compare this attitude to that of **Ray Lewis**, never shy to call attention to himself with his entrance dances and celebrations. It is tempting to pick Webster simply to affirm quiet virtue. On the other hand, as coach Yoast said in *Remember the Titans*, "You want to act like a star, you better give me star effort"; and star effort is exactly what Lewis gave as a Ravens linebacker. A two-time Defensive Player of the Year, he was the leading tackler on Baltimore's excellent defenses in every one of the 14 complete seasons he played. In 2000, the Ravens defense allowed 165 points, which remains a record low for a 16-game season. That D also gave up a record-low 970 rushing yards, a sign that guys were swarming to the football, and no one led a swarm better than Lewis.

Outside of football, the choice is **Jamaal Wilkes**, a quiet man whose chief means of calling attention to himself was the release of his jump shot, easily the most unusual stroke of any top gunner. Wilkes began with the ball over his shoulder before releasing it over his head. But it worked so well that famed Lakers announcer Chick Hearn referred to Wilkes shooting an open jumper as a "20-foot layup."

→ **THE VERDICT**

RAY LEWIS

THE DEBATE

WITH ALL DUE respect to **Harry Carson**, the Giants Hall of Famer, and also to longtime Broncos great **Randy Gradishar**, it is time to interrupt in this run of linebackers. The man breaking the streak, however, also was known to leave opponents black-and-blue.

Don Drysdale, the 1962 Cy Young winner, was baseball's leading practitioner of the beanball. At 6' 5", the temperamental sidearmer threw at batters frequently enough and with such purpose that SI once termed him "the meanest man in baseball." One of his contemporaries, Reds pitcher Jim Brosnan, quipped to the magazine that "Don's idea of a waste pitch is a strike." That take-no-prisoners approach marked Big D as he pitched on three World Series winners and threw a then-record 58 consecutive scoreless innings in 1968. Also, Drysdale was one of baseball's top hitting pitchers since Babe Ruth. In '65 Drysdale batted .300 (in 130 at bats), and he had two seasons in which he hit seven home runs, with OPSs of .852 and .839, respectively. (For perspective, Pete Rose's OPS was lower most seasons.)

The most curious trend at 53 is the collection of NBA big men who wore the number from the mid-1970s through the early '90s—and not so much at any other time. The class of the group is Hall of Fame enshrinee **Artis Gilmore**, and the resident jester is backboard-breaking **Darryl Dawkins**. Then, a run of random, middling big men: **Rick Robey**. **Mark Eaton**. **James Edwards**. **Alton Lister**. **Joe Kleine**. **Stanley Roberts**. Even the patron saint of random, middling big men, **Paul Mokeski**, pulled on the old 5-3 for one season of his spectacularly unspectacular 12-year career.

➤ THE VERDICT
DON DRYSDALE

SO YOU WANNA BE IN PICTURES?

In 1968 Disney came out with a movie about a living car, HERBIE. The Love Bug had number 53 on its side because writer/producer Bill Walsh was a fan of DON DRYSDALE. The number stuck through four big-screen sequels, including the 2005 edition starring Lindsay Lohan. . . . Herbie found more success with 53 than any NASCAR competitor. The only 53 to take the checkered flag was BOB BURDICK, in 1961.

CONTENDERS

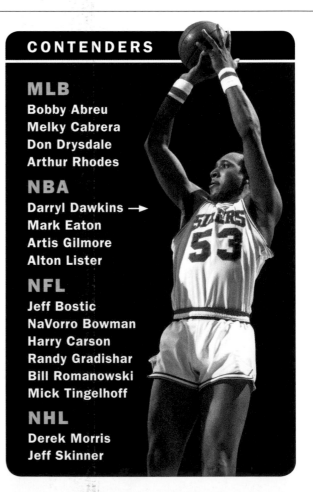

MLB
Bobby Abreu
Melky Cabrera
Don Drysdale
Arthur Rhodes

NBA
Darryl Dawkins ➤
Mark Eaton
Artis Gilmore
Alton Lister

NFL
Jeff Bostic
NaVorro Bowman
Harry Carson
Randy Gradishar
Bill Romanowski
Mick Tingelhoff

NHL
Derek Morris
Jeff Skinner

THE DEBATE

THE TOP TWO contenders at number 54 have this is common: These Hall of Famers both began their careers playing the wrong position. **Randy White** was a middle linebacker for his first two seasons in Dallas, before the team figured out that White would be more productive if he took a few steps forward and got down in a stance as a defensive tackle. (This was a time when you could have a 257-pound defensive tackle; similarly, Elliott Gould could be a leading man in the movies.) Still wearing his linebacker's number, White was named All-Pro seven times and was the most decorated member of Dallas's Doomsday defense in the 1970s. Those Cowboys went to three Super Bowls, winning once, against Denver, and White was named co-MVP of the game, along with Harvey Martin.

The edge, though, goes to **Rich (Goose) Gossage**, who began his career as a starter but flourished when he was sent to the bullpen. Back in the 1970s, relievers worked more innings than today, and Gossage was a setup man for himself. While Gossage's career save total of 310 is not overwhelming by today's standards, 125 of them took six outs or more, and in 24 he set down at least nine batters. Gossage has argued that he is better than Mariano Rivera because he worked harder for his saves, and while that claim is an overreach, it is fueled by a valid historical point. The intimidating Gossage is certainly one of the top five relievers ever.

Next up is **Brian Urlacher**, who also changed positions—from college safety to NFL middle linebacker. His ability to run, whether to tackle a back or cover a tight end, is what made him Defensive Player of the Year in 2005 and a near certainty for Canton.

➡ THE VERDICT

RICH GOSSAGE

DOING THE TEXAS TWO-STEP

The Cowboys are one of several NFL teams that don't retire numbers. They keep them in circulation and honor former greats with a Ring of Honor. Thus they celebrate two 54s: RANDY WHITE and five-time All-Pro linebacker CHUCK HOWLEY. Three other Dallas numbers are doubly represented: 22 (for Bob Hayes and Emmitt Smith), 43 (for Cliff Harris and Don Perkins) and 88 (for Michael Irvin and Drew Pearson).

CONTENDERS

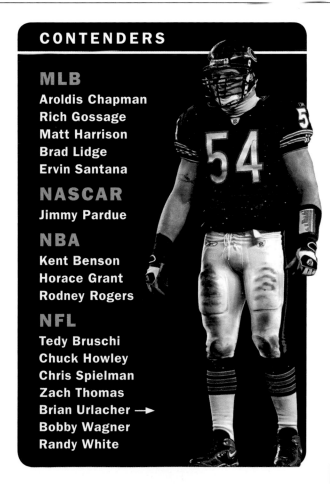

MLB
Aroldis Chapman
Rich Gossage
Matt Harrison
Brad Lidge
Ervin Santana

NASCAR
Jimmy Pardue

NBA
Kent Benson
Horace Grant
Rodney Rogers

NFL
Tedy Bruschi
Chuck Howley
Chris Spielman
Zach Thomas
Brian Urlacher ➡
Bobby Wagner
Randy White

55

THE VALUE OF A PAIR OF NICKELS

When he arrived at Georgetown, DIKEMBE MUTOMBO wanted number 15 but coach John Thompson preferred that his big men not wear numbers below 30. This is how the 7'2" center ended up with 55. Mutombo wore the number not only as a Hoya but also with each of his six NBA teams over his 18-year career. . . . Following Mutombo's path, another 7' 2" pivotman, ROY HIBBERT, wore 55 at Georgetown and is now sporting that numeral for the Pacers.

CONTENDERS

MLB
Kevin Appier
Orel Hershiser
Josh Johnson
Tim Lincecum
Hideki Matsui

NBA
Roy Hibbert
Dikembe Mutombo →

NFL
Derrick Brooks
Lee Roy Jordan
Willie McGinest
Matt Millen
Joey Porter
Junior Seau
Terrell Suggs

NHL
Sergei Gonchar
Larry Murphy
Keith Primeau

DO YOU PLACE more value on consistent excellence or one year of historic greatness?

Representing consistent excellence at this number are two linebackers who played in the 1990s and 2000s, **Derrick Brooks** and **Junior Seau** *(below)*. Brooks was named to 11 Pro Bowls and made All-Pro five times, and also won a Defensive Player of the Year award in '02, the season Tampa Bay won a Super Bowl. Seau had 12 Pro Bowls to his name and was a six-time All-Pro. The team success gives Brooks the slight edge. While Seau's Chargers did make it to one Super Bowl, with Seau being the unquestioned defensive star of the team (the second most notable name was safety Rodney Harrison, who was just a rookie) they were summarily carved up, allowing 49 points to the 49ers. Of course, when Brooks's Buccaneers won a Super Bowl, that defense also featured Warren Sapp, Ronde Barber and John Lynch.

But when the Dodgers and **Orel Hershiser** won the 1988 World Series, the righthander was undoubtedly the engine of victory. First, he capped off a regular season in which he threw 15 complete games by reeling off a streak of 59 consecutive scoreless innings. Then in the NLCS he won Game 7 by throwing a complete–game shutout against the Mets. In the World Series he beat Oakland twice. Here's what he had on his shelf when it was all over: an NLCS MVP award, a World Series MVP award and a Cy Young Award. What other pitcher has had a fall like that? None, ever. Of course it's an oversimplification to credit a team's success to one player—you may recall Kirk Gibson hitting a dramatic home run to win Game 1 of the Fall Classic—but Hershiser makes it darn tempting. His overall résumé features some historical unevenness. He went 23–8 his Cy Young year, and 19–3 a few seasons before that, yet his career win-loss record is only 204–150. He's not in his sport's Hall of Fame. But in his greatest season, he was as good as it gets.

➤ THE VERDICT
OREL HERSHISER

135

56

THE DEBATE

IF YOU HAD to build a linebacking crew out of players who wore just one number, the choice would be 56, just ahead of 52. The number boasts four Hall of Famers, including one pure category-killer.

We'll be playing a 4–3 defense in this fantasy, and manning the middle is eight-time All-Pro **Joe Schmidt**. The brainy leader of the Lions' defenses from 1953 through '65, he often is credited with being the first true "defensive quarterback" at the position. And we'll need his savvy to make the run defense work, because the rest of the guys are primarily known for their pass rushing. **Chris Doleman** was drafted as a linebacker but played most of his career at end, at which he piled up 150½ sacks. **Andre Tippett**, also on the squad, had 100 sacks for the Patriots.

But even with the Canton-quality credentials of these men, the star of this crew is **Lawrence Taylor**. LT is the NFL's only three-time Defensive Player of the Year. He retired with 132½ sacks (not including 9½ from his rookie season, before sacks were officially counted as stats) and also forced 33 fumbles, 10 of which he recovered. Behind the numbers is the real point, which is that Taylor is the most feared pass rusher the game has seen. "He has been known to wink and smile at his prey across the line, as if to warn, Ready or not, here I come!" wrote Jill Lieber in SI in January 1987, as Taylor's Giants were about to win the Super Bowl. That season, with a league-best 20½ sacks, Taylor was also named the league's Most Valuable Player. He is one of only two defensive players to win that award.

Could this imaginary group stop the run? With LT as a member, you have to like its chances.

➤ THE VERDICT

LAWRENCE TAYLOR

HOW PERFECTLY CURIOUS

From the department of kooky coincidences (or obvious conspiracies, take your pick): The signature accomplishments of four-time All-Star MARK BUEHRLE are his no-hitter for the White Sox against the Rangers in 2007 and his perfect game two years later against the Rays. In both games the umpire behind the plate was ERIC COOPER, and he, like Buehrle, was wearing number 56.

CONTENDERS

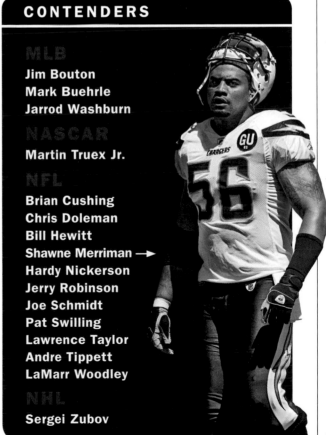

MLB

Jim Bouton
Mark Buehrle
Jarrod Washburn

NASCAR

Martin Truex Jr.

NFL

Brian Cushing
Chris Doleman
Bill Hewitt
Shawne Merriman ➤
Hardy Nickerson
Jerry Robinson
Joe Schmidt
Pat Swilling
Lawrence Taylor
Andre Tippett
LaMarr Woodley

NHL

Sergei Zubov

57

IF IT AIN'T BROKE, DON'T FIX IT

In 1938, the year he threw consecutive no-hitters, JOHNNY VANDER MEER wore 57 because the Reds were trying a consecutive numbering system: All players and coaches wore uniforms numbered between 35 and 67. The next year the Reds dropped the system and Vander Meer switched to 33. In 2013 the pitcher's hometown of Midland Park, N.J., honored the 75th anniversary of the feat by having their youth players wear 57.

CONTENDERS

MLB

Antonio Alfonseca
Chad Gaudin
Juan Guzman
Steve Howe
Darryl Kile
Francisco Rodriguez
Johan Santana
John Smiley
John Wetteland

NFL

Rickey Jackson
Tom Jackson →
Olin Kreutz
Clay Matthews
Bart Scott
Dwight Stephenson
Jeff Van Note

NHL

Tyler Myers
David Perron

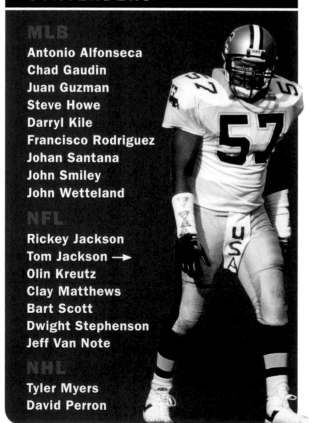

COMPARING A starting pitcher and an offensive lineman is like comparing the lead singer of a band to the guy working the soundboard. They are doing very different things, obviously. But one of them will be noticed only when he messes up.

When **Dwight Stephenson** *(below)* was manning the metaphorical soundboard as center for Dan Marino and the Dolphins, the quarterback didn't have to worry about the quality of his support. With the powerful yet nimble Stephenson at the controls, the Dolphins surrendered the fewest sacks in the NFL for six consecutive years. SI's Paul Zimmerman described Stephenson as "pure lightning" when naming the center to his All-Century team in 1999. The only pity of Stephenson's career is that a left knee injury brought him down after only six seasons as full-time starter.

Injuries have also hampered the career of **Johan Santana**. From 2004 through '06 the lefty from Venezuela put together as dominant a three-year stretch as you'll see. For the Twins he led the league each year in strikeouts, WHIP, ERA-plus and some other stats they haven't made up yet. He also earned two Cy Young Awards and then received his ultimate reward, negotiating a six-year, $137.5 million deal upon being traded to the Mets in 2008. His first season in New York was a good one (16–7 with a league-leading 2.53 ERA) but soon Santana's arm collapsed like a Bernie Madoff Ponzi scheme. Even Santana's throwing the franchise's first no-hitter, in 2012, turned out to be bittersweet: He was recently back from shoulder surgery and stayed in the game longer than he should have, pursuing history. Ten months later he underwent surgery again. But what he showed when he was healthy makes him the choice.

The number three finisher here, ironically, had a longevity the other two would envy. **Clay Matthews**, a four-time Pro Bowl linebacker in Cleveland, is known for playing in 278 games. Also, for being Clay III's dad.

THE VERDICT

JOHAN SANTANA

58

LET'S BEGIN TO praise one the toughest guys ever to strap on a football helmet by talking about a kicker: the Steelers' Roy Gerela. In Super Bowl X Gerela missed a field goal and immediately afterward Cowboys safety Cliff Harris began taunting him face mask to face mask. Pittsburgh's **Jack Lambert** didn't like that, and he did something about it. "We are supposed to be the intimidators," said Lambert, explaining why he came up behind Harris, lifted him and tossed him to the ground. But Lambert's true intimidation that day was leading a Steelers defense that sacked quarterback Roger Staubach seven times on the way to the second of four Super Bowls his teams would win.

Lambert, a relatively slim 6' 4" and 220 pounds, became one of the game's great tacklers because he played with intensity, viciousness and a cagey intelligence. The savvy could be masked, of course, by his on-field savagery, but it was why he was the Steelers' defensive captain, and it was also why he was named Defensive Player of the Year twice.

The second-best 58 is the explosive **Derrick Thomas**, who in one 1990 game sacked Seattle quarterback Dave Krieg seven times. Thomas had 126½ sacks in 11 seasons before dying less than a month after a car crash left him paralyzed from the waist down in 2000.

THE VERDICT
JACK LAMBERT

CONTENDERS

MLB
Jonathan Papelbon

NFL
Carl Banks
Jack Lambert
Wilber Marshall
Von Miller
Derrick Thomas
Jessie Tuggle

NHL
Kris Letang

HE IS TRULY IN THE MONEY

Whether you find the following anecdote amusing or annoying may reflect how you felt about the Occupy movement that has protested economic inequality—and was picking up steam, coincidentally, right about the time reliever JONATHAN PAPELBON signed with the Phillies in November 2011. His four-year contract was for $50,000,058, with the final digits being a nod the number he has worn throughout his career.

O.K., SO THAT DIDN'T WORK

Since JACK HAM's retirement after the 1982 season, the Steelers have issued number 59 once—to TODD SEABAUGH, a 1983 third-round pick out of San Diego State who had drawn comparisons to the Hall of Fame linebacker he had been slotted in to replace. Seabaugh, however, missed his rookie year with a back injury and after one season on the active roster as a reserve was done in the NFL.

THE DEBATE

THE ONLY HALL OF FAMER in any sport to wear 59 is the wonderfully named **Jack Ham**, who played alongside a man with whom he is sharing these pages, Jack Lambert. Like his Steelers colleague, Ham was not especially large, at 6' 1", 225 pounds, and legend has it that when he showed up for his first pro game, he had to talk his way past a security guard who did not believe he was a player. But Ham's speed and agility, and most of all his ability to diagnose a play and snuff it out, helped him intercept 32 passes, recover 21 fumbles and make six All-Pro teams.

From Ham it's a clear step down to the next man on the list, linebacker **Seth Joyner**. He was the lead linebacker on some excellent Eagles defenses led by coach Buddy Ryan and, later, coordinator Bud Carson. SI's Paul Zimmerman was so impressed by Joyner's work under Carson in 1991 that he named Joyner his NFL player of the year, offense or defense. Dr. Z said Joyner's ability to rush the passer and also cover receivers made him the glue of the D. Joyner obviously didn't enjoy Ham's level of decoration, but when he was at his best, he could soar.

Third pick is also a linebacker, **London Fletcher**. In the late '90s he was nicknamed "Dot-com" because, as it was explained, he was always "on-line with the opposition." The four-time Pro Bowler lasted 16 seasons, well into the 4G era and long enough to see his old nickname become a quaint anachronism.

→ **THE VERDICT**
JACK HAM

141

CHANGE OF ADDRESS

BY THE NUMBERS

Nearly every NBA great who went to college was able to carry over his school number to the pros—but in a handful of cases touted rookies were forced to make a switch

MAGIC JOHNSON 33 to 32

Magic led Michigan State to a national title as a 33, but with the Lakers those digits belonged to the great Kareem Abdul-Jabbar.

DAVE BING 22 to 21

With future Hall of Famer Dave DeBusschere wearing 22 for the Pistons, Bing checked down when he left Syracuse for Detroit.

BOB COUSY **17** to **14**

The Holy Cross star's college number was already taken by light-scoring Celtics forward Bones McKinney.

PETE MARAVICH **23** to **44**

The NCAA's alltime top scorer was prevented from keeping his LSU number by Hawks All-Star Lou Hudson.

BLAKE GRIFFIN **23** to **32**

Thanks to a preseason knee injury, Griffin never played an official game with his L.A. number-holder, Marcus Camby.

WES UNSELD **31** to **41**

Another big man, Ray Scott, blocked Unseld from wearing his Louisiville number in Baltimore.

THE DEBATE

IT'S MORE FUN to categorize **Otto Graham** as a 60 even though he switched to 14 for his last four seasons, if only because it's rare to see a quarterback wearing what is thought of today as a lineman's number. That old-time quarterback's number certainly matches the Chuck Taylor-ish shoes he is wearing in the opposite photo. Graham is so old school, in fact, that he was with the Browns when they were in the All-America Football Conference, which was notable for two reasons. One, it gave us the 49ers and the Browns. Second, it was the rare league dominated by a Cleveland team. All four AAFC titles were won by Graham's team in Cleveland.

When the Browns joined the NFL in 1950, they didn't skip a beat, winning a championship as Graham threw four touchdown passes in the title game. The Browns then lost the next three championship games before winning again in '54. In that game, he threw for three touchdowns and ran for three more. But simply making it to 10 consecutive title games is the stat that defines Graham as the ultimate winner.

Despite a generally thin group at number 60, the runner-up is an outstanding one: **Chuck Bednarik**, the last of the great two-way players. When the Eagles won the 1960 NFL championship, Bednarik played center and linebacker for 58½ minutes, sitting out only his team's kickoffs. Still he was fresh enough at the end to make a game-saving tackle of the Packers' Jim Taylor at the eight-yard line. That season Concrete Charlie also notably knocked out Frank Gifford with a hit for the ages. It's amazing that Bednarik could be voted the game's alltime center, as he was in '69, when his most famous plays weren't even on that side of the ball.

➤ **THE VERDICT**
OTTO GRAHAM

HIGH AND MIGHTY IN MONTREAL

It is unusual to see a goalie wearing such a lofty number, but JOSE THEODORE won the 2001–02 NHL MVP award wearing number 60. He ended up with the number in Montreal because his first choice, 33, which he had worn in juniors, had been taken off the market out of respect for Patrick Roy. Theodore originally saw 60 as temporary but after doing well and seeing kids wearing it, he has been a 60 for five teams.

CONTENDERS

MLB
Dave Heaverlo
Jon Rauch
Scott Schoeneweis

NASCAR
Geoff Bodine
Doug Cooper

NFL
Chuck Bednarik ➤
D'Brickashaw Ferguson
Otto Graham
Larry Grantham
Tommy Nobis
Chris Samuels
Otis Sistrunk
Max Unger
Bill Willis
Roy Winston

NHL
Jose Theodore

61

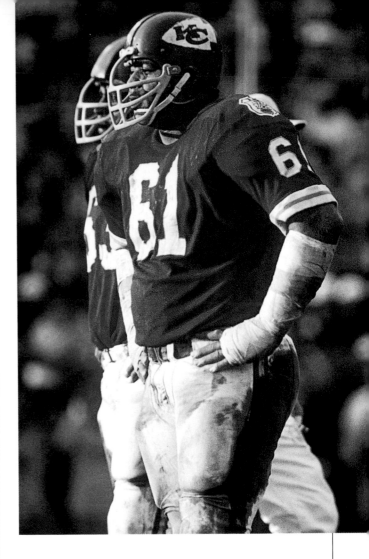

CONTENDERS

Bronson Arroyo
Livan Hernandez

Curley Culp
Bill George
Nick Hardwick
Nate Newton
Jesse Sapolu

Rick Nash

EXECUTING THE DOUBLE FLIP

When he joined the Marlins, pitcher JOSH BECKETT wanted to wear number 19, but it was taken by third baseman Mike Lowell, so Beckett flipped the numbers to 61. When he was traded to Boston before the 2006 season Beckett changed to 19, but then in '12 he had to switch back to 61 when he joined the Dodgers, where 19 had been retired for former second baseman and coach Jim Gilliam in 1978.

THE DEBATE

THE TOP CHOICES here are two Pro Football Hall of Famers who did their best work up the gut.

Curley Culp, who had been a collegiate wrestling champion at Arizona State, became a prototypical nosetackle in the NFL. Culp deftly employed his body-moving skills for a Chiefs team that won Super Bowl IV, with the defense holding the Vikings to seven points. Success followed Culp when he was traded to the Oilers. In Houston, he was named the NFL's defensive player of the year for 1975, and, despite having split his time between 61 and 78, he's the pick here.

The next man down is **Bill George**—the OBML, which stands for Original Bears Middle Linebacker. He's also a candidate for being the first true middle linebacker in football. Back in the day most teams used a five-man front, but George was among the first,

or some say *the* first, to step back and play away from the line. Whoever stuck whose chocolate in whose peanut butter, George certainly excelled at the new position, making All-Pro teams eight times.

While not a Hall of Fame–type player like Culp or George, a solid third place goes to righthander **Livan Hernandez**, who as a Marlins rookie took command of the 1997 baseball postseason, winning four games and being named NLCS and World Series MVP. Though he changed teams eight times, and his career won-loss mark is 178–177, he was ever a workhorse. He built a 17-season career, and he wore 61 at every stop.

→ **THE VERDICT**
CURLEY CULP

THE DEBATE

REMEMBER JUST a few years ago when it looked as if **Joba Chamberlain** was destined to be the next great Yankee? As a rookie in 2007, he appeared in 19 games, threw 24 innings and had an ERA of 0.38. But in the playoffs against Cleveland, the midges descended and the tiny bugs drained his magic. His career continued, decidedly less charmed. And so the debate for greatest 62 comes down to offensive linemen.

If you are to be known as an immortal offensive lineman, it helps to be part of a winning operation. None was more triumphant than the undefeated 1972 Dolphins, and at the center of their line was **Jim Langer**. Playing with fellow Hall of Famer Larry Little and Bob Kuechenberg, a six-time Pro Bowler, Langer helped others shine by efficiently taking care of his business. In that perfect season, he blocked without help on 497 of his 500 snaps. The four-time All-Pro handled his man and let others concentrate on theirs.

Second to Langer is guard **Guy McIntyre**, who won three Super Bowls in San Francisco. In 13 seasons with the 49ers, Packers and Eagles, his teams made the playoffs 12 times. The agile McIntyre was also one of the first lineman of his era to line up in the backfield on short runs. The Bears copied the move and turned Refrigerator Perry into a pop–culture phenomenon.

➤ **THE VERDICT**
JIM LANGER

ALWAYS CLOSE TO HIS HEART

It's a way to remember a friend. JOBA CHAMBERLAIN has worn numbers whose digits add up to 8 because that was the uniform number of Nate Raun, a childhood pal who died of brain cancer. Chamberlain's college number was 44, and in the minors he wore 53 and 62, which he took with him when he joined the Yankees. In 2012 Chamberlain pledged $62 for each strikeout to his foundation, Dream62.

63

THE DEBATE

ON A TEAM full of outlaws, **Gene Upshaw** was a straight man—a bright light in the Black Hole, if you will. He actually told Al Davis, before he was drafted in the first round out of Texas A&I, that the Raiders were "too rowdy" and that he preferred to play somewhere else. The Oakland owner, impressed with the way Upshaw spoke his mind, took him anyway. The guard became a leader on the team for a decade and a half, from 1967 to '81, as the Silver and Black won two Super Bowls and Upshaw made seven Pro Bowls and five All-Pro teams. After his playing days Upshaw distinguished himself as the first African-American head of a pro players union, running the NFLPA for a quarter century.

Upshaw stands out here among a fertile field that includes several clear-cut Hall of Famers. Next down the list is **Willie Lanier**, who, like Upshaw, was a pioneer: He was the first African-American star at middle line-backer. He was a Chiefs rookie in 1967, and inserting him in the lineup was a no-brainer, because he quickly became one of the best ever. Thickly built at 6'1", 245 pounds, Lanier earned the nickname Contact with his ferocious hitting, and with mates Curley Culp and Buck Buchanan made Kansas City into a defensive force.

Just behind, by a smidge, is **Lee Roy Selmon**, who faced the burden of being the first player taken by the Buccaneers in their expansion season of 1976. Strong enough to play defensive tackle and fast enough to play end, he stood out on some awful teams. (Tampa Bay won seven total games over its first three seasons.) When he finally had some help around him in 1979, Selmon was named Defensive Player of the Year. Injuries cut short his career at age 30.

→ **THE VERDICT**
GENE UPSHAW

148

A DISPLAY OF LOYALTY

The Hurricanes wore patches adorned with 63 during the 2011–12 season to honor center JOSEF VASICEK after he was one of 44 to die in a plane crash carrying players, coaches and staff of his Russian club, Lokomotiv. Vasicek, who played seven seasons and was on Carolina's 2006 Stanley Cup team, was issued 63 at his first training camp and never switched.

CONTENDERS

MLB
Rafael Betancourt
Kevin Gregg
Justin Masterson

NFL
Justin Blalock
Larry Cole
Brad Edelman
Jay Hilgenberg
Ernie Holmes
Willie Lanier
Kirk Lowdermilk
Mike Munchak
Jeff Saturday
Lee Roy Selmon
Fuzzy Thurston
Gene Upshaw

NHL
Brad Marchand →
Mike Ribeiro

HE BLOCKED for six running backs who each rushed for more than 1,000 yards in a season, and provided protection for five quarterbacks, all of whom threw for more than 3,000 yards in a season. The stats for offensive lineman are few, but when you look at the skill players around him it's clear that many benefited from the services of **Randall McDaniel**, a left guard who was a vital cog in some prolific Vikings offenses, most notably in 1998 when Minnesota scored a dazzling 34.8 points per game. For his efforts McDaniel was named to 12 consecutive Pro Bowls, from '89 through 2000, and he's our top choice here.

McDaniel is in the Hall of Fame and **Jerry Kramer** is not, which is a source of irritation to Green Bay fans who believe that the guard, a finalist for induction nine times, has been discriminated against because 10 Packers from those 1960s championship teams are already enshrined. True or not, the five-time All-Pro was an essential figure in the signature offensive play of those teams, the Lombardi sweep. Kramer also blocked for Bart Starr on his winning sneak in the Ice Bowl, one of the most famous touchdowns in NFL history. And he could kick too, making 29 career field goals. Kramer may be deserving, but he's only third here, behind Hall of Famer **Dave Wilcox**, a premier coverage linebacker for the 49ers with seven Pro Bowl appearances.

THE VERDICT

RANDALL MCDANIEL

CONTENDERS

NASCAR
Elmo Langley

NFL
Jim Burt
Ken Gray
Jeff Hartings
Jerry Kramer
Randall McDaniel
Tom Rafferty
Jack Reynolds
Dave Wilcox

HE SHOWED A BIT OF INTEREST

Nineteen NHL players have worn number 64, but Mike Commodore is not among them, much to the disappointment of an ardent group of petitioners. In 2011, after Commodore signed with the Red Wings, tech fans pushed for the defenseman to wear the number to honor the Commodore 64, a seminal home computer in the '80s. Commodore tweeted that he would consider it but ultimately stuck with his number, 22.

65

A TALL ORDER TO PHIL

When he joined the Yankees in 2007, PHIL HUGHES requested a jersey number ending in 5. Some were retired (5 for Joe DiMaggio, 15 for Thurman Munson) or taken (25 by Jason Giambi, 35 by Mike Mussina, 45 by Carl Pavano). So the 6'5" righthander ended up with 65. In his second season Hughes briefly switched to 34, but after a poor, injury-racked run he handed it off to Xavier Nady and returned to 65.

THE DEBATE

IN THE SPEECH he gave at his Hall of Fame induction, **Gary Zimmerman** spoke of "The Curse"—which to him meant playing with a great quarterback, as he had done with John Elway for five seasons in Denver, after spending seven years in Minnesota. The tackle found protecting Elway to be an overwhelming responsibility. "What happens is the night before the game you get little or no sleep knowing that if you screw up you will forever be known as the guy who lost the franchise," Zimmerman said. "Like clockwork I would wake up between 4:00 and 4:30, flop around for a while and finally get up."

Both Zimmerman and Elway made it to Canton, a testament to Zimmerman's having done his job, and done it consistently well. Not surprisingly he was named to the NFL's All-Decade teams for both the 1980s and '90s.

"He can dance with a finesse guy like Derrick Thomas," linemate Dave Widell explained to SI in '94. "Then, if he's up against a power end like Richard Dent or Chris Doleman, he'll play a power game."

Elvin Bethea was, like Zimmerman, consistently excellent, manning defensive end for the Oilers for 16 seasons. Bethea was named to eight Pro Bowls while playing on some awful teams, and also some very good ones that provided the Steel Curtain–era Steelers with some fiery battles in the late 1970s. Bethea has said that his role model as a lineman was Deacon Jones and while, like Jones, he has no official sack totals, the unofficial count places him around 105.

→ **THE VERDICT**

GARY ZIMMERMAN

66

AN OUTRAGE TO THE FAITHFUL

When fledgling Flames defenseman T.J. BRODIE was issued number 66, fans of MARIO LEMIEUX were irate and campaigned for Brodie to change numbers. He said he would do it when he felt more established and he did, switching to 7 after his first season. . . . SCOT POLLARD, the colorful NBA center, wore 66 for with the Celtics in 2007–08. Some joked that he chose a number with two 6s because the league wouldn't let him wear one with three 6s.

CONTENDERS

MLB
Logan Ondrusek
Yasiel Puig →

NFL
George Andrie
Bill Bergey
David Diehl
Conrad Dobler
Alan Faneca
Kevin Gogan
Gene Hickerson
Joe Jacoby
Larry Little
Tom Nalen
Ray Nitschke
Randy Rasmussen
Billy Shaw
Bulldog Turner

NHL
Mario Lemieux

IT'S HARD TO think of an athlete who has meant more to his franchise, and his city, than **Mario Lemieux** has to the Penguins and to Pittsburgh.

To begin, he was simply a team-elevating prodigy—in his debut game in 1984, he stole the puck from the Bruins' Ray Bourque and scored on his very first shot. He would lead the NHL in scoring six times and guide the Penguins to two Stanley Cups, in '91 and '92.

But Lemieux's narrative took on unexpected, and unwanted, depth. In 1993, while seeking a third consecutive Stanley Cup, he discovered he had Hodgkin's disease, which required radiation treatment that caused him to miss two months. He returned that season and keyed a 17-game winning streak. But the coming seasons brought back surgeries and more games missed. He retired in '97, though his story was far from over.

In 1999, with the Penguins near financial ruin and owing Lemieux more than $30 million in deferred salary, he decided to buy the team, in the process saving the franchise from possibly abandoning Pittsburgh. A year later Lemieux returned to the ice as a player-owner, and scored in his first game back. Though he retired again in January 2006, he still had one more assist to make: By helping the Penguins reach a deal for a new arena, he secured their presence in the Steel City for decades to come.

It's dumb luck that two of the best players in all of the 60s both wore 66. Otherwise, **Ray Nitschke** *(above)* would be an easy winner. On a Packers defense with five other Hall of Famers, Nitschke was the snarling leader. The middle linebacker brought a passion to the field that told all too well of a painful upbringing. Orphaned at age 13, he treated his team like family, and he played with an urgency that was intensely personal. Nitschke, like Lemieux, became a fixture in his team's city after his playing days, watching games at Lambeau, enjoying the community.

➤ **THE VERDICT**

MARIO LEMIEUX

67

THE DEBATE

HIS FATHER worked as a human cannonball at the circus. He'd get shot out once a weekday, and twice on Saturdays. "I asked him about it, and he said that when you come out of the cannon you're unconscious," **Bob Kuechenberg** told SI in 1982, toward the end of his NFL career. "Then at the apex of your flight you gather your senses and your instinct is to reach out and try to get to the net quicker. That's where it's important to know what you're supposed to do. The trick is to stay relaxed, to never reach out, because you could land wrong in the net and break something."

Kuechenberg played like a man who came from tough stock. His pro career got off to a rough start when he was cut by the Eagles and then the Falcons before he ever played a down. But the offensive lineman eventually latched on with the Dolphins and thrived in Miami for 14 seasons. He was part of the undefeated 1972 campaign, but his greatest display of toughness came a year later. After fracturing his forearm and missing the final game of the '73 season, he had a pin inserted to hold the bone together and rejoined the team for the playoffs. With one solid arm he fended off the Vikings' Alan Page, keeping the great defensive tackle from being a factor in the Dolphins' 24–7 Super Bowl VIII win.

Kuechenberg is the choice here ahead of **Reggie McKenzie**, a Bills offensive lineman who blocked for O.J. Simpson in 1973, when the back gained 2,003 yards, and is also favored over **Russell Maryland**, the No. 1 overall pick in the 1991 draft. Maryland never quite lived up to that status, but the defensive tackle did start for three Super Bowl winners and make one Pro Bowl during his five seasons in Dallas.

→ THE VERDICT

BOB KUECHENBERG

THINKING BIG, BUT NOT THAT BIG

Current Jets and former Blackhawks forward **MICHAEL FROLIK** came gently to 67. The Czech Republic native explained, "Someone told me I should pick out some big number. Number 68 [worn by countryman Jaromir Jagr] is untouchable, so I went one lower." . . . The only NBA 67 is M O E B E C K E R of the Detroit Falcons. In 1947 Becker took 107 shots, making 19. Neither the number nor the Falcons caught on.

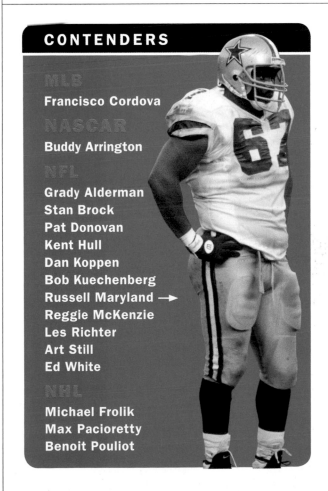

CONTENDERS

MLB
Francisco Cordova

NASCAR
Buddy Arrington

NFL
Grady Alderman
Stan Brock
Pat Donovan
Kent Hull
Dan Koppen
Bob Kuechenberg
Russell Maryland →
Reggie McKenzie
Les Richter
Art Still
Ed White

NHL
Michael Frolik
Max Pacioretty
Benoit Pouliot

155

68

HE HAD a mullet and sped like a bullet. By the time **Jaromir Jagr** was 20, playing alongside Mario Lemieux, he had already won the Stanley Cup twice. Then he added gold at the 1998 Olympics. He ran off four consecutive scoring championships from '97–98 through 2000–01, though critics noted that his desire to score goals seem to far outweigh his dedication to preventing them.

Thus was it the case that in 2005, when Jagr led the Czech national team to a title at the hockey world championships, SI hockey writer Michael Farber saw it as Jagr's crowning moment, because Jagr had shown guts, playing against doctor's advice with a broken pinkie on his left hand. Supportive fans showed up with their little fingers wrapped in gauze. "The artiste with the soft hands and the sometimes too-soft game had never done anything that spoke so eloquently to the essence of his sport," Farber wrote. Coincidence or not, the next season Jagr had a career-best plus-minus of 34.

Finishing second to Jagr is **Russ Grimm**, a Redskins offensive lineman and a member of a unit known as The Hogs. It says here that any group of guys that can compel other guys to dress in women's clothing and plastic pig snouts is one that you ignore at your peril. The Hogs lineup changed over the years but Grimm was there for all three Super Bowl wins and is the only one enshrined in the Hall of Fame.

► THE VERDICT

JAROMIR JAGR

CONTENDERS

NFL
Rubin Carter
Joe DeLamielleure
Gale Gillingham
L.C. Greenwood
Russ Grimm
Kevin Mawae
Will Shields
Kyle Turley

NHL
Jaromir Jagr

REMEMBERING THE REVOLUTION

A native of the Czech Republic, JAROMIR JAGR wears 68 in honor of the Prague rebellion of 1968. His grandfather died that year after being jailed for refusing to work on his farm for free.... L.C. GREENWOOD wore 68 in four Super Bowl wins, but the most distinctive aspect of his uniform was his gold shoes. After an ankle injury he had to wear high-top shoes and, to make them look better, L.C. had them painted gold.

THE DEBATE

THE TOP PLAYER at number 69, by a good long way, is **Jared Allen**. He gets as big a jump on this field as he's ever had on any offensive lineman, and that's saying something. The speedy Allen has led the NFL in sacks twice, with 15½ in Kansas City in 2007 and again with 22 for the Vikings in '11. The '11 total was just shy of Michael Strahan's record 22½ sacks in 2001, and Allen didn't need Brett Favre to fall on the ground and wait to be touched down.

The pickings are slim at this number because, perhaps wanting to avoid locker-room taunts, not many players have chosen to wear 69. The choice for second from among a group of modestly decorated NFL players is Bengals nosetackle **Tim Krumrie**, who starred in the second most memorable play (after Joe Montana's game-winning pass) of Super Bowl XXIII. In Krumrie's play, the nosetackle was chasing Roger Craig and heard a crunch, but kept going and made the tackle. Only when Krumrie tried to rise did he realize that the crunch was both his tibia and fibula snapping. When the gruesome replay was shown, many in the Bengals' family area wept. Doctors needed to insert a 15-inch rod into Krumrie's leg. The most amazing detail? Despite the hideousness, the two-time Pro Bowler didn't miss a game—not next season, not ever in his 12-year career. Krumrie is tough enough to handle number 69.

➤ THE VERDICT
JARED ALLEN

CONTENDERS

NFL
Jared Allen
Jordan Gross
Tim Krumrie
Henry Melton
Woody Peoples
Jon Runyan
Mark Schlereth
Will Wolford

NHL
Andrew Desjardins

AN INNOCENT REQUEST?

When he joined the Lakers in 1998, DENNIS RODMAN, according to rumor that is both popular and all-too-believable, asked to wear number 69 but his request was denied. If true, there are a couple points of consolation for the Worm. One is that he is card number 69 in both the '95–96 Topps and '98–99 Bowman basketball sets. The other is that he wasn't singled out: No NBA player has ever worn 69.

ALL IN THE FAMILY

BY THE NUMBERS

When athletes follow in the footsteps of parents or siblings, they often carry more than the same DNA. Check out the family resemblance in these uniform pairs

ARCHIE & PEYTON MANNING 18

The number Archie (left) rode to gridiron glory at Ole Miss has been Peyton's in Indianapolis and now Denver.

BOBBY & BARRY BONDS 25

Barry (right) wore 24 in honor of his godfather Willie Mays in Pittsburgh, then followed his dad's example as a Giant.

KEN GRIFFEY SR. & JR. 30

When Junior (right) joined his dad's old team in Cincinnati in 2000, he also switched to Ken Sr.'s number.

CHERYL & REGGIE MILLER 31

The sister-and-brother Hall of Famers wore the same number in college; when Reggie left UCLA he kept it with the Pacers.

THE BOONES 8

Ray, Bob, and Aaron (top to bottom) had a three-generation link.

THE ZELLERS 40

Luke, Tyler and Cody (top to bottom) adhere to a fraternal code.

THE TOP FOUR players are really quite similar. They all earned their stripes fighting it out in the NFL trenches, and they did it long ago, though not quite in ancient times (after leather helmets, but before Chris Berman). While they all are in the Pro Football Hall of Fame, their names don't reverberate at the Jim Brown-Dick Butkus level. The most famous is **Art Donovan**, the longtime Colts defensive lineman who became a late-night talk show regular. When Donovan passed away in 2013, the news stories showed him with David Letterman as much as they did with Gino Marchetti. But the choice—above Donovan, **Ernie Stautner** and **Rayfield Wright**—is **Sam Huff**.

The Giants linebacker also made an impression through the media, one that helped define the NFL as it grew in popularity. He was the subject of a 1960 CBS television special titled *The Violent World of Sam Huff*, which was hosted by newsman Walter Cronkite. Huff was featured in part because he played in a media center, but he was also the heart of a Giants defense that reached six NFL title games, winning one. The native of West Virginia coal country was rugged enough to take on Jim Brown and nimble enough to intercept 30 balls in his 13 seasons. Unabashedly brutal, "rough, tough Sam Huff" was the personification of a league just beginning to fascinate America.

▶ **THE VERDICT**

SAM HUFF

CONTENDERS

NFL
Art Donovan
Leon Gray
Sam Huff
Logan Mankins
Jim Marshall
Ernie Stautner
Bob Whitfield
Rayfield Wright

NHL
Braden Holtby

SO WHAT IF IT'S A TECHNICALITY?

The only Steelers player ever to have his number retired is ERNIE STAUTNER, a scrappy defensive lineman who played in Pittsburgh from 1950 to '63. While Stautner was great and beloved, the distinction owes to an unofficial change in team policy regarding number retirements. The digits of other notables—such as Franco Harris's 32, Terry Bradshaw's 12 and Jack Lambert's 58—are merely out of circulation.

71

CONTENDERS

NASCAR
Bobby Isaac

NFL
Willie Anderson
Tony Boselli
Walter Jones
Alex Karras
Charles Mann
Jason Peters

NHL
Evgeni Malkin

HOW TO REACH THE MOTOR CITY

It sounds like a set of travel directions: If you want to go from Iowa to Detroit, take 77 to 71. That's how it happened for Detroit offensive tackle RILEY REIFF, a 2012 first-round pick out of Iowa. He wore number 77 in college and switched to 71 when he became a Lion. More than half a century earlier, Karras had also worn 77 at Iowa, and when he was drafted by the Lions in the first round, he too switched to 71.

THE DEBATE

IT IS OFTEN the case that defensive linemen enjoy more celebrity and glamour than their counterparts on the offensive line. The number 71 provides an exaggerated example, as the top two choices are a defensive lineman who parlayed his football success into a long career in show business and an offensive lineman whose name is comparatively obscure, even though he played more recently.

People see **Alex Karras** every time someone cues up the clip of Mongo punching a horse in the 1974 movie *Blazing Saddles*. But the man was a heck of a football player before he ever took his tough guy act to the screen. Strong and quick, he was named to the 1960s NFL All-Decade team despite laboring for mostly unimpressive squads in Detroit and missing a season when commissioner Pete Rozelle suspended Karras and Packers back Paul Hornung in 1963 for placing bets on NFL games (featuring other teams, not their own). Still, he's the choice.

Walter Jones, however, is a strong second. Jones was what every team wants when it spends a high draft pick on a left tackle. After taking Jones sixth overall in 1997, the Seahawks didn't worry about their quarterback's blind side for the next decade. The four-time All-Pro was also part of a line that helped Shaun Alexander reel off five straight 1,000-yard rushing seasons.

Keep an eye out for **Evgeni Malkin**. The young Penguins center already has led the NHL twice in points and was the postseason MVP during Pittsburgh's 2009 Cup run.

→ **THE VERDICT**
ALEX KARRAS

72

THE DEBATE

SOME BELOVED players wore number 72. There's **William (the Refrigerator) Perry**, a good defensive tackle who became a great novelty act when he joined the Bears backfield as a blocker and then a scorer. The Fridge had four touchdowns in 1985, including a one-yard run in the Super Bowl. While Perry had a fun, girth-related nickname, a better 72 had a height-inspired moniker that was just as good: **Ed (Too Tall) Jones.** The 6' 9" Cowboy was a defensive star on the great Dallas teams of the '70s and early '80s. In what (looking back) feels like a true '70s move, Jones left football at the height of his prime to take up boxing. Too Tall did well, sort of, winning all six of his fights against opponents who were pretty much stiffs. But such was the intrigue that all of his bouts were nationally broadcast on CBS. He then returned to football, and was a three-time Pro Bowl selection. Going strictly by coolness, Too Tall would be the choice, even over the Fridge.

But the selection for 72 is another lineman, albeit one with more staying power: **Dan Dierdorf**. The Michigan product had a long and sometimes rocky run as an analyst on NFL broadcasts, but there is no denying his credentials as a right tackle. From 1974 to '76 his St. Louis Cardinals allowed the fewest sacks in the NFL, including a then record-low eight sacks in '75, and in '77 and '78 his line was the best in that category in the NFC. Dierdorf was voted to the Pro Bowl every year of that stretch, nearly unanimously most years, and the Cardinals' line's run of statistical excellence ended with Dierdorf's '79 knee injury. He is the only player enshrined in Canton (his birthplace, by the way) to wear 72 as his primary number and a clear top pick here.

➤ **THE VERDICT**
DAN DIERDORF

HE WAS KNOWN FOR THE TRIPLE

The best NBA player to wear number 72 was also the only one to do so: **JASON KAPONO**. The swingman wanted to wear 24 when he was traded to the 76ers in 2009, but that number was retired for Bobby Jones. So Kapono, a three-point specialist, tripled his old number—and then shot his worst three-point percentage to date that season, and was even worse the next year. No wonder he switched to 28 for his last pro season.

CONTENDERS

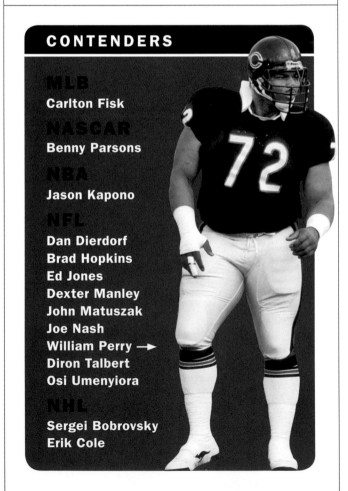

MLB
Carlton Fisk

NASCAR
Benny Parsons

NBA
Jason Kapono

NFL
Dan Dierdorf
Brad Hopkins
Ed Jones
Dexter Manley
John Matuszak
Joe Nash
William Perry ➤
Diron Talbert
Osi Umenyiora

NHL
Sergei Bobrovsky
Erik Cole

73

THE DEBATE

FOR READERS OF a certain age, the SI cover of Aug. 3, 1981, was memorable for a couple of reasons. First, it featured an offensive lineman, which was and is a rarity. More notable was the bold headline: THE BEST OFFENSIVE LINEMAN OF ALL TIME.

The lineman in question was **John Hannah**. The story inside was both a profile of the Patriots mainstay and a quest by its author, Paul Zimmerman, to determine the best ever at the position. "John has something none of the others ever had," New England general manager Bucko Kilroy told Dr. Z. "And that's phenomenal, repeat, *phenomenal*, lateral agility and balance, the same as defensive backs. You'll watch his man stunt around the opposite end, and John will just stay with him. He'll slide along like a toe dancer, a tippy-toe." And this was a guard, Kilroy said, who on other plays would be "positively annihilating" a foe who dared to attack him straight up.

The number 73 has belonged to many outstanding linemen. If any could challenge Hannah's spot here, it would be **Larry Allen**. He was a six-time All-Pro for the Cowboys, and he made the NFL's All-Decade teams in both the 1990s and the 2000s. Allen helped Emmitt Smith become the NFL's alltime leading rusher; late in Allen's career, he also cleared the way for Frank Gore to set a 49ers season rushing record.

In the three-plus decades since the Hannah cover appeared, some would say that Anthony Muñoz eclipsed him as the best ever. Allen and Muñoz are close, but not close enough for Allen to overtake Hannah. When you declare a man the greatest ever, you don't crawl back off that limb without overwhelming motivation.

➤ THE VERDICT

JOHN HANNAH

FLIPPING FOR CASEY

The best of the handful of baseball players to wear 73 (usually for a season or two) was pitcher KENNY ROGERS. The 219-game winner reversed the digits of his standard 37 when he joined the Mets in 1999 because that number was retired for manager Casey Stengel. The only baseball player to make a lengthy career with 73 was pitcher RICARDO RINCON, who wore it for 11 seasons and five teams, including the Mets in 2008.

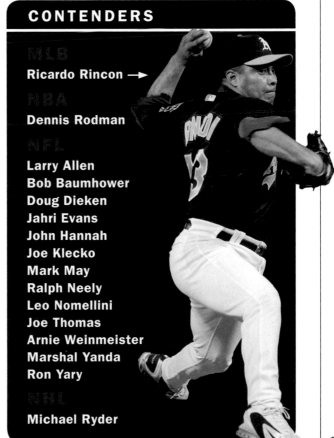

CONTENDERS

MLB
Ricardo Rincon ➤

NBA
Dennis Rodman

NFL
Larry Allen
Bob Baumhower
Doug Dieken
Jahri Evans
John Hannah
Joe Klecko
Mark May
Ralph Neely
Leo Nomellini
Joe Thomas
Arnie Weinmeister
Marshal Yanda
Ron Yary

NHL
Michael Ryder

THE DEBATE

THE VIRTUE of constancy is a hallmark of many of the greats who have worn number 74. **Henry Jordan**, a stalwart of the Green Bay defensive line during the Lombardi years, missed only two games in his first 12 NFL seasons. That makes him a positive shirker compared to **Merlin Olsen**, who sat out just two games in his 15 years as one quarter of the Rams' Fearsome Foursome. Then there's **Bruce Matthews**, who played guard, tackle and center for the Houston Oilers. When he retired, he held the record for most games played (296) by any position player. Or consider the mark of consistency attached to Chargers offensive lineman **Ron Mix**: In 10 seasons with San Diego, he was called for holding just twice.

These men are all Hall of Famers, as is the choice at this number, **Bob Lilly**. The Cowboys' defensive tackle, who was the franchise's first-ever draft pick, in 1961, played in every one of Dallas's 196 regular-season games during his 14-season career. But what's more impressive about "Mr. Cowboy" is that he remained a beacon of excellence as Dallas rose from league doormat to perennial contender. Lilly, wrote SI's Tex Maule, "is one of the very few men who, merely by his personal contribution, can establish the whole character of a game." Opposing coaches complained of having to spend half their prep time game-planning to stymie Lilly's penetration at the point of attack. When the Cowboys inaugurated their Ring of Honor, the first number they celebrated was Lilly's. While Ring numbers are not automatically retired—Dez Bryant wears Michael Irvin's old 88, for example—74 has not circulated. Bob Lilly is the only Cowboy ever to have worn it.

➤ **THE VERDICT**
BOB LILLY

TALK ABOUT A HOME UNIFORM

Growing up in Curaçao KENLEY JANSEN's street address was 74, which is why the Dodgers closer chose the number. The fifth-year man is one of only five major leaguers to wear the number and he already has worn it the longest. . . . PAUL COFFEY wore 77 for seven teams, but switched to 74 for his final season, in Boston in 2000–01, presumably in deference to Ray Bourque (who hadn't yet retired).

CONTENDERS

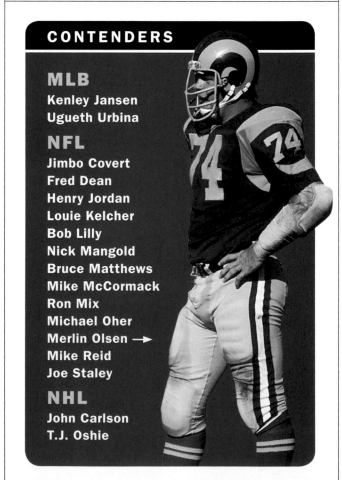

MLB
Kenley Jansen
Ugueth Urbina

NFL
Jimbo Covert
Fred Dean
Henry Jordan
Louie Kelcher
Bob Lilly
Nick Mangold
Bruce Matthews
Mike McCormack
Ron Mix
Michael Oher
Merlin Olsen ➤
Mike Reid
Joe Staley

NHL
John Carlson
T.J. Oshie

75

THE DEBATE

IT WOULD BE hard to declare 75 one of the greatest numbers in this book, given that it's been worn by so few athletes outside of football. But based on the football group alone, 75 may have been worn by the toughest group. Consider some of the men who've sported it, including **Jonathan Ogden**, the 6′ 9″ road grader of the Ravens' offensive line, and **Forrest Gregg**, whom Vince Lombardi once called the best player he ever coached. But what really boosts the toughness factor for 75 is its presence on the backs of two of the most intimidating players the NFL has ever produced: **Deacon Jones** and **Mean Joe Greene**.

Though Jones played before sacks were an official statistic, one estimate places his career total at 173. Beyond numbers, there is pain. Jones's signature move was the head slap. And the slaps often came loaded: He told SI in 1999 that he had a metal plate cut to fit his hand, which he then wrapped with a cast: "That's what you got upside your head, every 30 seconds." Fearsome indeed.

The choice here, though, is Greene, a two-time NFL Defensive Player of the Year who led the front-line charge on the vaunted Steel Curtain. Of the many stories about Greene's intensity, a favorite comes from early in Mean Joe's career. The Steelers were losing in Philadelphia. Greene felt he was repeatedly being held and he was fed up. So on the next play, before the center could snap the ball, Greene snatched it out of his hands, stood up and tossed a spiral into the stands, then stomped to the sidelines. The Steel Curtain was the baddest defense the NFL ever has seen, and Mean Joe set its tone.

▶ THE VERDICT
JOE GREENE

LONG (AND SHORT) SHELF LIFE

A's and Giants pitcher BARRY ZITO said he chose to wear number 75 because he liked the way the tops of the 7 and the 5 created a shelf under his name. . . . When he joined the Mets in 2009, closer FRANCISCO RODRIGUEZ, who had worn 57, switched to 75 because Johan Santana was already wearing 57. K-Rod went back to his old digits when he was traded to the Brewers in 2011.

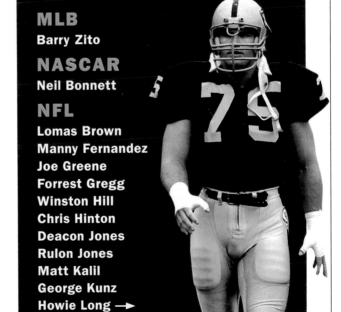

CONTENDERS

MLB
Barry Zito

NASCAR
Neil Bonnett

NFL
Lomas Brown
Manny Fernandez
Joe Greene
Forrest Gregg
Winston Hill
Chris Hinton
Deacon Jones
Rulon Jones
Matt Kalil
George Kunz
Howie Long ⟶
Jonathan Ogden
Stan Walters
Vince Wilfork
Fred Williams

76

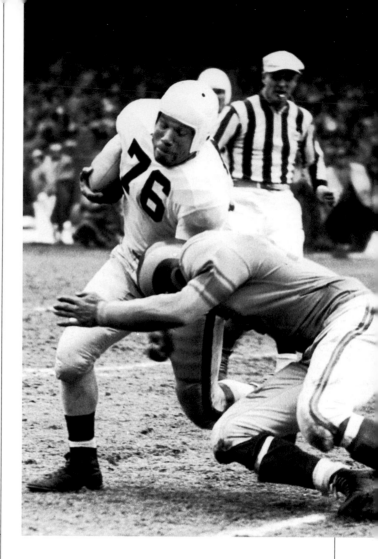

HEY, IT MATCHES THE LOGO!

It's fitting that the only NBA player to wear number 76 played for the 76ers. But the symmetry doesn't end there: The player was SHAWN BRADLEY, the 7'6" center drafted second overall in 1993. After two-plus seasons that were big only in their scale of disappointment, Philadelphia traded Bradley, and for the rest of his career he wore numbers (44, 45) that were more about blending in than standing out.

THE DEBATE

CLEVELAND FANS, this one is for you. Gather round, grab some Polish Boy sandwiches and make a bonfire out of the old LeBron James jerseys you haven't already burned. Because this debate comes down to two Browns legends: **Lou Groza** and **Marion Motley**.

Groza, a tackle and a placekicker, was a face of the franchise for the two decades he played in Cleveland. (The last years, from 1961 to '67, he was a kicker only). But he excelled at both his tasks. Six times he was an all-league blocker but, as his nickname suggests, "the Toe" was more influential as a kicker. Playing in a day when most teams didn't devote roster spots to kicking specialists, Groza was one of the few who attempted, and made, long-distance kicks, and twice he set new records for field goals made in a season. When he retired, he was the NFL's alltime leading scorer.

Groza would be a fine choice, but Motley is a better one. Besides being one of the toughest fullbacks ever to play the game, Motley was a barrier-breaker. In 1946 when at age 26 he joined the Browns in the AAFC, he became one of the first four African-American players in pro football. He was a physical runner and a load to bring down, with a per-carry average of a ridiculous 5.7 yards. The 232-pounder was also a peerless pass-protector. Coach Weeb Ewbank once told SI's Paul Zimmerman, "[Motley] takes the romance out of the blitz."

Cleveland retired 76 for Groza. But the Browns haven't been a model of football perspicacity for a while now. Their lead need not be followed.

→ THE VERDICT

MARION MOTLEY

THE DEBATE

IT IS TEMPTING to award this number to **Ray Bourque** simply because of his reverence for numbers.

For the first eight years of the 21 he spent as a Boston defenseman, Bourque wore number 7, which had previously been worn by Phil Esposito. At Esposito's retirement ceremony Bourque, the Bruins captain, skated up to Esposito and surprised him by pulling off his jersey to reveal a second jersey with a new number, 77, underneath. Bourque surrendered his 7 to Esposito as the Garden crowd thundered to the rafters. The moment so moved Esposito that he returned to Boston when Bourque, a 19-time All-Star and five-time winner of the Norris Trophy, had his 77 retired by the Bruins in 2001.

Bourque's competitor, though, is **Red Grange**, who gets extra points for carrying 77 through college and the pros—and for kick-starting America's favorite league. At Illinois the Galloping Ghost became one of the most famous athletes of his day, once scoring four touchdowns in the first 12 minutes of a game against Michigan. Then the halfback took that college fame and helped bring legitimacy to the fledgling NFL. Grange not only starred for the Bears, but he also participated in barnstorming tours, using his celebrity to draw fans to these events. His 77 is retired with the Illini and the Bears, and he owns it here too.

 **THE VERDICT**

RED GRANGE

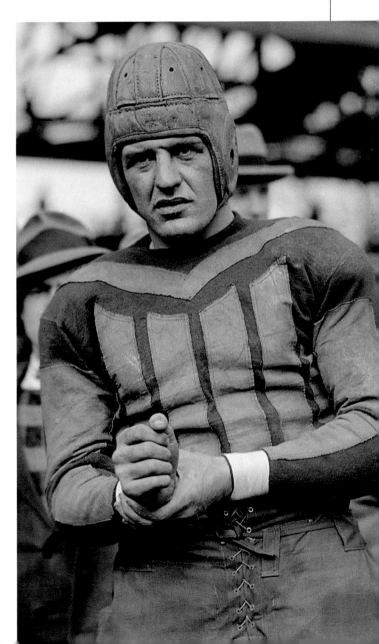

CONTENDERS

NFL

Lyle Alzado
Red Grange
Jim Jeffcoat
Karl Mecklenburg
Jim Parker
Willie Roaf

NHL

Ray Bourque
Paul Coffey
Pierre Turgeon

IT LOOKED GOOD WHEN HE DID IT

Shawn Bradley wasn't the only big man to match his height and number: 7' 7" GHEORGHE MURESAN did it in Washington and New Jersey. . . . IVAN RODRIGUEZ wore 77 for one season. He had switched from his customary 7 to 12 with the Yankees, where 7 is retired for Mickey Mantle. In Houston the 7 jersey was retired for Craig Biggio. Pudge tried 12 but opted for 77, saying, "I was just missing my number."

78

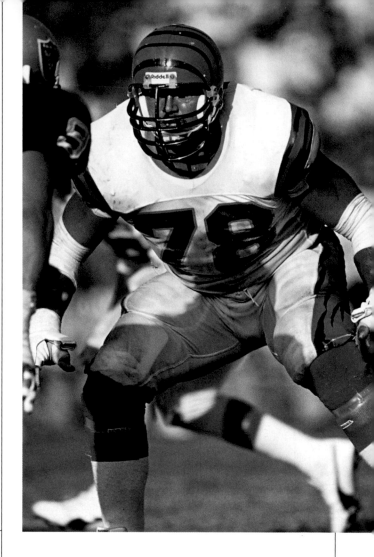

CONTENDERS

NFL

Bruce Armstrong
Bobby Bell
Matt Birk
Ryan Clady
Stan Jones
Anthony Muñoz
Art Shell
Jackie Slater
Bruce Smith
Richmond Webb
Dwight White

WHAT DOES A GUY HAVE TO DO?

BRUCE SMITH **had 171** of his record 200 sacks up in Buffalo, but the Hall of Famer's number, while out of circulation, has yet to be officially retired there. The only Bills number to be retired so far is Jim Kelly's 12. . . . 77 and 78 are known in mathematics as a Ruth-Aaron Pair, where the sums of the prime factors of two consecutive numbers are equal. The name was chosen because 714 and 715 are an example of it.

THE DEBATE

THE MAJORITY OF matchups in this book are hypothetical, but this one lived on turf as well as on paper. **Anthony Muñoz**, the supremely talented left tackle, did take on **Bruce Smith**, the official sack leader several times, never with more at stake than in the 1988 AFC championship game between Muñoz's Bengals and Smith's Bills. Smith was on the verge of winning the battle that day, as he blew past Muñoz for two sacks early, but a leg injury hobbled Smith and he was shut out the rest of the game. "I think if that hadn't happened," said Smith of the injury, "I would have probably had the best game of my life, and it probably would have been his worst. I felt like nobody could stop me." But Smith was indeed halted, and the Bengals won 21–10.

Smith once told SI, in praise of Muñoz, "What's amazing is that he does everything right." Muñoz returned the respect, including Smith on the short list of the best ends he had ever faced. Both men are highly decorated, with Muñoz having been named an All-Pro nine times to Smith's eight. Smith was a two-time Defensive Player of the Year; three times Muñoz was named the league's top offensive lineman. Smith was named to All-Decade teams in the 1980s and '90s. Muñoz was named to the NFL's 75th anniversary alltime team.

If there's a difference between these greats, it is, in two words: Reggie White. And maybe two more: Deacon Jones. While Muñoz is the game's best tackle ever, Smith slots behind White and possibly Jones as best defensive end. This is what gives Muñoz the slightest of edges.

THE VERDICT

ANTHONY MUÑOZ

THE DEBATE

THE MOST REMARKABLE number associated with **Roosevelt Brown**'s uniform is not, in truth, the one on the back, which was 79. More shocking is Brown's waist measurement, which was a mere 29 inches. And he was 6' 3" and 255 pounds. When Jerry Seinfeld lied about his waist size on his TV show, he pretended to be a 31, and he couldn't block Newman without the help of a closed door. Yet the swift Brown was one of the great blockers of his day. A 27th-round pick out of Morgan State, he made nine Pro Bowl teams for the Giants, pulling around from his tackle position and leading the charge for Frank Gifford and an array of other New York backs.

Brown is one of two football Hall of Famers at 79. The other is 6' 9" **Bob St. Clair**, a 49ers mainstay who played the same position as Brown at around the same time with somewhat less decoration (five Pro Bowls) and no particular distinction to his waist size. So let's skip over him to our third man, and the best pass rusher to wear 79, **Harvey Martin**. He was the NFL's Defensive Player of the Year in 1977 when he had an unofficial 20 sacks. In Super Bowl XII he had two sacks and helped fluster Broncos quarterback Craig Morton into four interceptions. His Cowboys held Denver to 10 points and Martin took co-MVP honors with linemate Randy White.

➡ THE VERDICT
ROOSEVELT BROWN

CONTENDERS

NFL

Roosevelt Brown
Jacob Green
Jim Lee Hunt
Gary Johnson
Jim Lachey
Harvey Martin
Bob St. Clair
Erik Williams

NHL

Andrei Markov

IN DALLAS, 7+9 EQUALS 4

HARVEY MARTIN wasn't the only Cowboy to do well in 79. It was also worn by offensive tackle ERIK WILLIAMS, who like Martin made four Pro Bowls. . . . Phillies reliever JUSTIN DE FRATUS is the rare baseball player to choose 79. He asked for it because it was his Arizona Fall League number, reportedly reassuring the Phillies that he would not ask for a lower number a few weeks later. He did stick with it—for two years, before trying 30 in 2014.

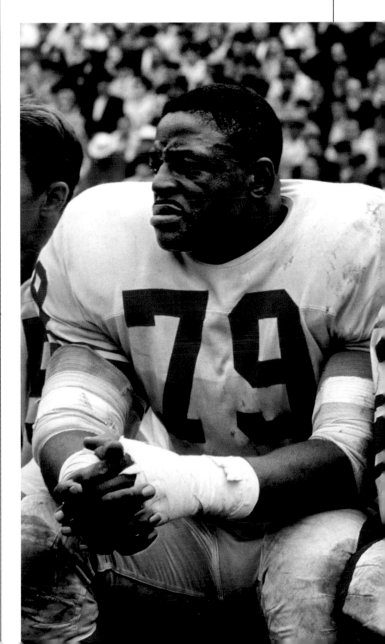

For the few athletes who have become crossover stars, being multitalented has usually—but not always— meant choosing more than one number

BO JACKSON 34 and 16

The Heisman winner from Auburn was able to wear his college number as a Raiders running back but not as a Royals outfielder.

DAVE DEBUSSCHERE 22

The Hall of Fame forward also pitched two seasons (with a 2.90 ERA) for the White Sox—and carried his number from NBA to MLB.

DANNY AINGE 44 and 2

At BYU he wore 22: when doubled it was his Celtics number, when truncated it was his Blue Jays identifier.

DEION SANDERS 21

As if Prime Time wasn't recognizable enough, he wore his familiar number in both the NFL and MLB.

MARK HENDRICKSON 27 and 42

At 6'9" he tried the NBA (and Nos. 14 and 42) before switching to baseball (and Nos. 43, 30, 27 and 31).

BRIAN JORDAN 40 and 33

He played safety for the Falcons for three seasons, then spent 15 years as an outfielder with four MLB teams.

80

THE DEBATE

THERE IS NO number with greater representation in the Pro Football Hall of Fame than 80. Eight men wore it as their primary number, ranging from old-timers such as Steelers cornerback **Jack Butler** to longtime Vikings receiver and 2013 inductee **Cris Carter**. Even among this throng of alltime greats, however, there is really no argument as to the most deserving: It has to be **Jerry Rice**, who rewrote the record book for receivers. Rice had 14 1,000-yard seasons, made 1,549 receptions and scored an absurd 208 touchdowns. His career receiving yards total 22,895, while the next nine players on the list are all bunched between 13,777 and 15,934. (That top 10 includes three other 80s, by the way—**Isaac Bruce**, **James Lofton** and Carter.) The 10-time All-Pro was a winner too—his 49ers triumphed in three Super Bowls, and Rice also played in a fourth one late in his career for Oakland. In a position that has become associated with divas, he channeled his fierce competitiveness into the game-by-game task of defining greatness for the duration of his career.

Among this crew of Hall of Famers there is also a runner-up: **Kellen Winslow**. The Chargers tight end was among the best ever at his position, jockeying for the privilege with John Mackey and Tony Gonzalez. Also, Winslow delivered one of the most memorable performances in league history. In a classic playoff game against Miami in 1982, Winslow caught a record 13 passes and came in on special teams to block what would have been a game-winning field goal. The three-time All-Pro had to be helped off the field by teammates after the game, having lost more than 10 pounds but also having etched an enduring image of athletic perseverance.

➤ **THE VERDICT**
JERRY RICE

CONTENDERS

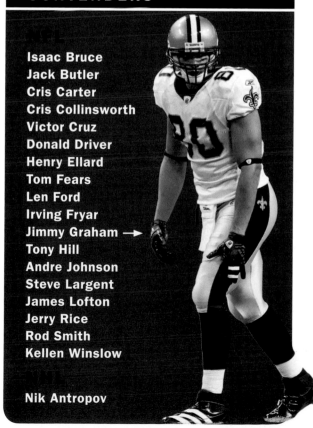

NFL

Isaac Bruce
Jack Butler
Cris Carter
Cris Collinsworth
Victor Cruz
Donald Driver
Henry Ellard
Tom Fears
Len Ford
Irving Fryar
Jimmy Graham ➤
Tony Hill
Andre Johnson
Steve Largent
James Lofton
Jerry Rice
Rod Smith
Kellen Winslow

NHL

Nik Antropov

THANKS, BUT NO THANKS

The most returned 81 jersey is that of AARON HERNANDEZ. After his arrest on murder charges in 2013, the Patriots offered free exchanges for the tight end's gear, and 1,200 fans took them up on it. . . . On a nicer note: In May 2013 a third-grade student in Chicago, taking a math test, answered that "9×9" equaled "Hossa," for the number of MARIAN HOSSA, the All-Star Blackhawks right wing. She got credit for the answer, as well as a moment of viral fame.

CONTENDERS

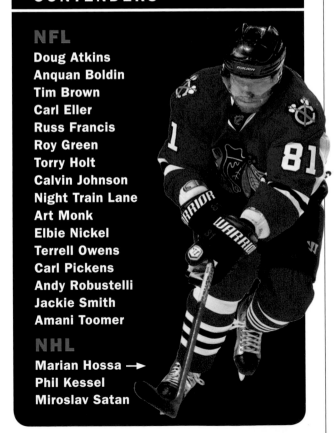

NFL

Doug Atkins
Anquan Boldin
Tim Brown
Carl Eller
Russ Francis
Roy Green
Torry Holt
Calvin Johnson
Night Train Lane
Art Monk
Elbie Nickel
Terrell Owens
Carl Pickens
Andy Robustelli
Jackie Smith
Amani Toomer

NHL

Marian Hossa →
Phil Kessel
Miroslav Satan

WHAT IF the choice here was **Terrell Owens**, and just to double-down on the endorsement of this often reviled figure we illustrated the pick with a photo of the 49ers receiver celebrating a touchdown on the star in the middle of Texas Stadium, preening, about to be clocked by Cowboys safety George Teague for one of the acts of provocation that defined Owens's career?

Personality aside, T.O. *(below)* does have a strong argument for being the best 81: He has the most receiving yards of any player not named Jerry Rice, and he's third on the alltime list in receiving touchdowns and sixth in receptions. While he seemed to live by the motto of Dylan McKay from *Beverly Hills, 90210*—"May the bridges I burn light the way"—he did remain spectacularly loyal to 81 as he wore out his welcome in one NFL stop after another.

Owens stands an excellent chance of joining the six 81s currently in the Hall of Fame, and he has set a high bar statistically for Detroit's **Calvin Johnson**, the best receiver in today's game. Johnson may take over this number one day, but for now the leader of the pack is another Lion, **Dick (Night Train) Lane**, the most intimidating cornerback of his day and a guy who probably would have relished the challenge of covering T.O. or Megatron. Lane wore such a high number because he originally tried out for the Rams as a wide receiver, but he moved to defensive back because the team already had two future Hall of Famers at wideout, Tom Fears and Elroy (Crazy Legs) Hirsch. Lane, though, played cornerback with a physicality that suggests that defense was in fact his true calling. He would lock onto receivers, bump them down the field and then attack those who had the temerity to catch the ball. His signature takedown was the Night Train Necktie, and if that sounds like a finishing move out of professional wresting, that's pretty much what it was. The neck-high tackle was eventually banned by the league. Bottom line: You didn't want to get hit by the Night Train.

THE VERDICT
NIGHT TRAIN LANE

THE QUICKEST way to explain **Raymond Berry** is to say that he was to Johnny Unitas what Jerry Rice was to Joe Montana; that is, the favorite target of an all-time great. Berry led the NFL in receptions three times, and had 12 catches in The Greatest Game Ever Played, the Colts' overtime win in the 1958 NFL championship.

What makes Berry a distinctive figure, however, is not his stats but his story. Unlike most top receivers, he was not particularly fast—in fact, one of his legs was shorter than the other. But the fierce competitor made up for his lack of speed by doing everything else perfectly. He developed new receiving routes and practiced them tirelessly, until his body moved as precisely as the line in a play diagram. A telling stat: He fumbled once in 13 seasons, a reflection of the tenacity with which he went about every aspect of his business.

The race for second comes down to two tight ends, **Jason Witten** and **Ozzie Newsome**. While Witten's stats are much better than Newsome's, the Brown was regarded as the second-best tight of his era, behind Kellen Winslow. The same cannot be said of Witten, who ranks behind Tony Gonzalez and Antonio Gates, at least. Witten is a strong candidate for the Hall of Fame, assuming his numbers still seem as remarkable five years after he retires. But Newsome is already there, and he slots ahead of Witten.

THE VERDICT

RAYMOND BERRY

CONTENDERS

NFL
Raymond Berry
Dwayne Bowe
Ozzie Newsome
Mike Quick
Jimmy Smith
John Stallworth
John Taylor
Jason Witten

NHL
Martin Straka

THE MONSTER'S WARTIME MINDER

The name of the only MLB player to wear 82, JOHNNY LAZOR, may not resonate, but he is a footnote to history. When Ted Williams went off to World War II, it was Lazor who took his spot in leftfield in Boston.... JOHN STALLWORTH, who wore 82, was the 82nd player selected in the 1974 draft—and one of the four Hall of Famers taken that year by Pittsburgh. (The others were Lynn Swann, Jack Lambert and Mike Webster.)

83

CONTENDERS

NFL

Flipper Anderson
Deion Branch
Mark Clayton
Willie Gault
Ted Hendricks
John Jefferson
Heath Miller
Andre Reed
Golden Richards
George Sauer
Wes Welker

GOOD THINGS COME IN THREES

He was initially issued number 84, which LEE EVANS didn't like because the Bills' 2004 first-round pick (whose full name is Lee Evans III) had had a 3 on his jersey at every level. Buffalo had not been circulating number 83 out of respect to ANDRE REED, but Evans received permission from Bills owner Ralph Wilson, and a thumbs up from Reed himself, to wear the number of the seven-time Pro Bowler and '14 Hall of Famer.

THE DEBATE

AMID THIS run of pass catchers, it is time to honor a linebacker—albeit one with dimensions more suited to a tight end or even a wide receiver. **Ted Hendricks** was 6' 7" and 220 pounds, which earned him the nickname "the Mad Stork," and he never wanted to bulk up. "When I grab 'em they're grabbed," the linebacker told Raiders owner Al Davis. "I don't need weights." Though Hendricks began his career as a Colt and played a year with the Packers, he found his greatest success in Oakland, winning three Super Bowls. (He won a fourth with Baltimore.) The eight-time Pro Bowl linebacker was also a weapon on special teams, blocking 25 field goals or extra points, and a great many punts as well.

The top challenger is nearly a foot shorter than Hendricks—5' 9" receiver **Wes Welker**. Like Hendricks,

Welker flourished at the third stop on his NFL tour. After one game in San Diego and nearly three full seasons in Miami, he was traded to New England and, in partnership with quarterback Tom Brady, blossomed, with five 100-catch seasons. Three times Welker led the league in receptions. Those numbers set Welker ahead of the other receiving 83s, including **John Jefferson**, who opened his career with three 1,000-yard seasons in San Diego before being traded to Green Bay in 1981 because of a contract dispute. Instead of Dan Fouts, his quarterback was now Lynn Dickey. Right at the point his career Welker found his quarterback, Jefferson lost his. It's a big reason one is ahead of the other.

THE VERDICT

TED HENDRICKS

181

84

THE DEBATE

IT IS EASY to be distracted from the accomplishments of **Randy Moss**, who famously declared, "When I want to play, I'll play" to justify his in-game mini-vacations. Then there was his pantomime of a mooning of the Packers faithful after he scored a touchdown in a wild-card contest at Lambeau Field. With another player that incident might have been ascribed to the intensity of the Vikings-Packers rivalry, but with Moss it was another piece of evidence that the receiver didn't fully respect the game.

But all that shouldn't obscure how dynamic a player he was. When he came into the league in 1998, he was compared with Michael Jordan. It didn't seem fair, the way he would leap above his defenders and pluck the ball from the air. Even though he started only 11 of 16 games in his rookie season, he led the league in touchdowns—the first of five times he would accomplish that feat. He averaged 19.0 yards per catch, which is amazing considering he caught 69 balls that year.

After leaving Minnesota in 2005, Moss had his down years (in Oakland, wearing 18) and then more up years (in New England, wearing 81, where he set the single-season touchdown receptions mark of 23 in 2007) before a desultory finish in Tennessee, Minnesota and San Francisco (all 84). Despite so many bumps in the road, he finished his career second alltime in receiving touchdowns behind Jerry Rice with 156.

The second pick for 84 is a strong one—**Shannon Sharpe**, who won two Super Bowls in Denver and a third with the Ravens. He rewrote the record book for tight ends—until Tony Gonzalez came in and did a really heavy edit.

➤ THE VERDICT
RANDY MOSS

REMEMBRANCE OF THINGS PAST

He wore 4 most of his career but CHRIS WEBBER switched to 84 in Detroit in 2006–07. With 4 retired for Joe Dumars, Webber chose 84 in part it because it's a football number, and he played tight end as a Detroit high schooler. . . . J.T. SNOW, who wore 6 with the Angels and Giants, switched to 84 for his final season, with the Red Sox, to honor his late father, former Rams receiver JACK SNOW.

CONTENDERS

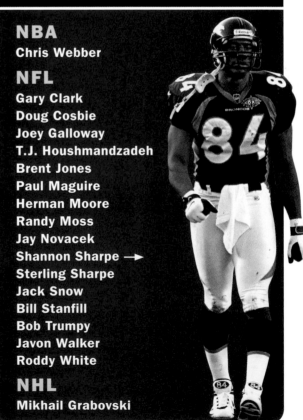

NBA
Chris Webber

NFL
Gary Clark
Doug Cosbie
Joey Galloway
T.J. Houshmandzadeh
Brent Jones
Paul Maguire
Herman Moore
Randy Moss
Jay Novacek
Shannon Sharpe ➤
Sterling Sharpe
Jack Snow
Bill Stanfill
Bob Trumpy
Javon Walker
Roddy White

NHL
Mikhail Grabovski

85

THE COMMITMENT is impressive. It's tempting to give **Chad Johnson**, formerly Chad Ochocinco, the nod here simply for changing his last name to his uniform digits. His on-the-field argument is not a horrible one either. In 2006, he led the NFL in receiving yards and over the course of his career earned six Pro Bowl nods. But if the focus is more on play, then the names to consider are **Nick Buoniconti** and **Antonio Gates**, two players whose mark on football history extends beyond novelty.

The case for Gates is that he is a transformative figure. The increased emphasis on pass-receiving tight ends had already begun before he arrived in the NFL in 2003. But Gates, an undrafted free agent who played basketball at Kent State but not football, became the face of a revolution. He caught 81 passes and 13 touchdowns in his first season as a starter, 89 and 10 in his second, on his way to eight consecutive Pro Bowls.

Buoniconti, however, made another kind of history. After being named to six AFL All-Star teams, he became the biggest name on the Dolphins' "No-Name Defense" that won two Super Bowls and went undefeated in 1972. Buoniconti, then 32, was the oldest player on his side of the ball by five years, and as the middle linebacker he was responsible for improvising adjustments to the defensive calls that came in from the sideline. That defense allowed 12.2 points per game, best in the NFL, and it shut down Washington in the Super Bowl. Could Buoniconti have covered the 6' 4" Gates? At 5' 11", he surely would have found it a tall order. But then, the Notre Dame alum overcame a lot to become a winner and a Hall of Famer. Nick might well have found a way.

➤ THE VERDICT

NICK BUONICONTI

BACK TO WHERE IT ALL STARTED

The point guard began his career wearing number 1 during his All-Star seasons with the Hornets and returned to it later with the Clippers. But when **BARON DAVIS** was playing with Cleveland in 2010–11 and New York in '11–12, he switched his uniform number to 85. Nearing the end of his 13-year career, he wanted to honor his grandparents, who raised him and who lived on 85th Street in Los Angeles.

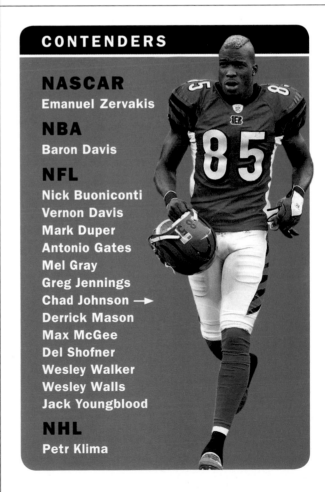

CONTENDERS

NASCAR
Emanuel Zervakis

NBA
Baron Davis

NFL
Nick Buoniconti
Vernon Davis
Mark Duper
Antonio Gates
Mel Gray
Greg Jennings
Chad Johnson →
Derrick Mason
Max McGee
Del Shofner
Wesley Walker
Wesley Walls
Jack Youngblood

NHL
Petr Klima

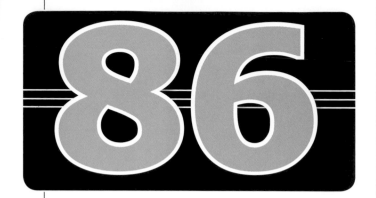

THERE MAY WELL be heated debate in the room of writers who will get together at Super Bowl LI to determine whether **Hines Ward** belongs in the Hall of Fame. But he's the top 86 here, ahead of two men already enshrined: **Dante Lavelli**, a Browns receiver from 1946 to '56, and **Buck Buchanan**, a Chiefs defensive tackle from '63 to '75.

Buchanan is Ward's most serious competition. The defensive tackle was the first overall pick of the 1963 AFL draft, out of Grambling. He had great size—he was 6' 7", 270 pounds—and exceptional speed and agility. In '67 alone he batted down 16 passes. Three years later Buck spearheaded the defense when the Chiefs defeated the Vikings 23–7 in Super Bowl IV.

Ward also knows of big-game heroics. He caught five balls for 123 yards in Super Bowl XL, scored the fourth-quarter touchdown that put the contest out of reach and was named the game's MVP. Beyond that one big day, Ward had exactly 1,000 career receptions and six seasons with more than 1,000 yards receiving. He also was a nasty blocker, so dangerous that an opposing linebacker needed to keep his head on a swivel, watching out for Ward when he didn't have the ball. The mere threat of a collision kept opposing defenses off-balance. No one would say he was a prototype receiver. Everyone would call him a winner.

→ THE VERDICT
HINES WARD

CONTENDERS

NFL
Fred Barnett
Verlon Biggs
Buck Buchanan
Gary Collins
Earl Faison
Antonio Freeman
Todd Heap
Dante Lavelli
Stanley Morgan
Hines Ward
Charle Young

THE ROSTER OF THE UNDEAD

When he appeared as a zombie on the TV show *The Walking Dead*, HINES WARD's makeup artists placed an 86 on the back of his head made of "bruises". . . . The first NBA player to wear 86, briefly, was SEMIH ERDEN, for the Celtics in 2011. The second was CHRIS JOHNSON, also for the Celtics in '11. Johnson, called up from the D League, hastily reported to Boston and was handed an old Erden jersey with a new name patched on.

87

THE DEBATE

SIDNEY CROSBY arrived with great fanfare as the most heralded NHL rookie since Wayne Gretzky. (Somewhere Eric Lindros is saying, "What about me?") Crosby lived up to the hype almost immediately, winning the league scoring title as a teenager and leading his team to a Stanley Cup by the time he was 21. But then he missed huge chunks of time due to a concussion, and his play since has leveled off a tiny bit. Which presents the problem of assessing a career that is still in progress. Is it too soon to declare the Kid, before he has reached 30, the best at this number, ahead of two NFL Hall of Famers, **Willie Davis** and **Dave Casper**?

Well, no, and it's not because of any projections about the future. Crosby is the choice at number 87 based on what he already has accomplished. Beyond the titles and the trophies (Ross, Hart, Richard and the Lindsay, twice) he has been the Man in his sport (or at worst, the co-Man, along with Alex Ovechkin). Davis and Casper, as great as they were, never had to carry that burden. Davis was the top pass rusher on the Packers championship teams of the '60s, but the linchpin of that defense was Ray Nitschke. Casper was a top tight end in his day, but those loaded Raiders teams had many prime timers (Ken Stabler, Ted Hendricks, Jack Tatum, Fred Biletnikoff, Gene Upshaw, Art Shell). The Kid has had to grow up faster than his elders.

THE VERDICT
SIDNEY CROSBY

CONTENDERS

NFL
Dave Casper
Dwight Clark
Ben Coates
Willie Davis
Rob Gronkowski
Claude Humphrey
Jordy Nelson
Reggie Wayne

NHL
Sidney Crosby

HE WAS BORN THAT WAY

This is certainly a simple explanation: SIDNEY CROSBY wears 87 because his birthday is 8/7/87.... Crosby isn't the only top NHL pick to wear the number. PIERRE TURGEON, the first choice in the 1987 draft, wore 77 for 17 seasons in Buffalo and four other NHL stops. But when he joined the Avalanche for the 2005–06 season, Turgeon switched to 87 because 77 had been retired in Colorado for Ray Bourque.

88

THE DEBATE

A CONTEST FOR the greatest number ever worn by NFL pass catchers would come down to 80 and 88. The Hall of Fame–caliber receivers who have donned 88 include **Marvin Harrison**, **Lynn Swann** and **Michael Irvin**, and the tight ends include two of the greatest to play the position. There's **John Mackey**, the first consistent deep threat at the position and a powerhouse who could bulldoze defenders either after the catch or when he was run blocking. And there's **Tony Gonzalez**, who holds positional records for receptions and touchdowns by a country mile. Among this group, Gonzalez stands out as the top choice.

But in an upset at this pass-catching number the choice is a defensive tackle, **Alan Page**. What made Page so great? It certainly wasn't size, as he was 6' 4" and only 245 pounds. But he attacked with speed and relentless effort that made Minnesota's Purple People Eaters click. When Page joined a front four that already featured Carl Eller and Jim Marshall, the Eaters set off on a feast that included four trips to the Super Bowl, with Page earning All-Pro honors six times along the way. Most impressively, in 1971 he was named NFL MVP, one of only two defensive players to be so honored. (The other is Lawrence Taylor.) Argument over.

There's a curious side trend at 88: Several men who wore number showed great ambition outside football. Swann ran as the Republican candidate for governor of Pennsylvania in 2006. Mackey's legacy as a players' labor leader may equal that of his work on the field. Page earned a law degree and became a state Supreme Court justice in Minnesota. Again, it's Page who impresses the most—case closed.

➤ **THE VERDICT**
ALAN PAGE

TWO IS NOT BETTER THAN ONE

In his second stint with the Celtics, in 2005, ANTOINE WALKER wore number 88 for two games, before he was able to reclaim his original number, 8, from rookie Al Jefferson, who surrendered it freely. . . . DALE EARNHARDT JR. began racing car number 8, but when he left DEI and moved to Hendrick Motorsports for the 2008 season, he couldn't keep the number and made the switch to 88.

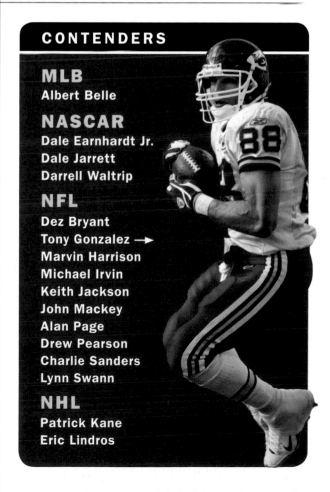

CONTENDERS

MLB
Albert Belle

NASCAR
Dale Earnhardt Jr.
Dale Jarrett
Darrell Waltrip

NFL
Dez Bryant
Tony Gonzalez ➜
Marvin Harrison
Michael Irvin
Keith Jackson
John Mackey
Alan Page
Drew Pearson
Charlie Sanders
Lynn Swann

NHL
Patrick Kane
Eric Lindros

89

THE DEBATE

ISN'T IT WEIRD how, after having so many greats at 88, the competition slims out one digit later? Everyone wants to hang with the double-snowmen at 88, but 89 is just another number.

Don't tell that to our top choice, **Mike Ditka**. Before he was Da Coach, a TV commentator or a steakhouse owner, he was a force at tight end. Consider Ditka's first pro season, 1961, in which he scored 12 touchdowns and had 1,076 receiving yards. He won Rookie of the Year, stretching the field in a way that was rare for tight ends of his day, while blocking with the intensity that still comes through in his temperamental demeanor. He made the Pro Bowl in each of his first five seasons, and was the first tight end to be enshrined in Canton. It was his abilities, and not just his persona, that allowed him to become one of the signature characters of the NFL.

Next on the list is **Gino Marchetti**, one of the game's great tough guys. In 1969 Marchetti was voted the best defensive end of football's first 50 years. The Baltimore Colt's defining innovation was relying on footwork as much as force; Marchetti explained that he had spent a year playing offensive tackle, and he had the most trouble with the guys who went around him instead of trying to bowl him over.

Mention must be made of **Mark Bavaro**, the tight end who played on two Super Bowl teams with the Giants, and memorably dragged Ronnie Lott down the field during a game against the 49ers in 1986. Unfortunately, a degenerative knee condition in his sixth season ended Bavaro's time with the Giants, and his effectiveness. He would come back as an 83 with the Browns and an 84 with the Eagles, but he was never the same.

➤ **THE VERDICT**
MIKE DITKA

THE FIRST AND THE LAST

In 1989 he became the first hockey player to defect from the Soviet Union to the United States, and **ALEXANDER MOGILNY** commemorated the date by wearing 89 as he became a four-time All-Star right wing with the Sabres and Canucks. . . . The Bears have the most retired numbers in the NFL, with 14, but before retiring 89 for MIKE DITKA in 2013, they said his would be the last.

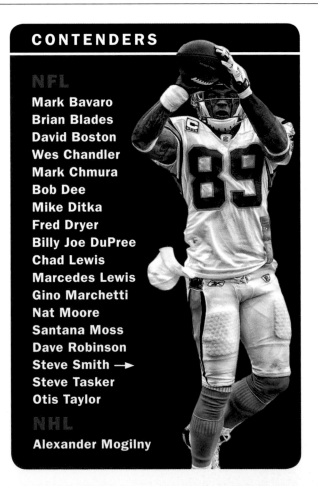

CONTENDERS

NFL

Mark Bavaro
Brian Blades
David Boston
Wes Chandler
Mark Chmura
Bob Dee
Mike Ditka
Fred Dryer
Billy Joe DuPree
Chad Lewis
Marcedes Lewis
Gino Marchetti
Nat Moore
Santana Moss
Dave Robinson
Steve Smith ➤
Steve Tasker
Otis Taylor

NHL

Alexander Mogilny

Not all sports figures wear numbers when they compete—but many who don't have made an article of clothing as distinctively theirs as any uniform

TIGER WOODS'S RED SHIRT

Woods has worn this hue on Sundays throughout his career, after his mother told him that it was his "power color."

PAYNE STEWART'S KNICKERS

Players wore plus-fours in tribute to Stewart after the two-time U.S. Open winner died in a 1999 plane crash.

JERRY TARKANIAN'S TOWEL

If you argue that a towel is not clothing, you never saw the way the UNLV hoops coach kept his attached to his person.

BOBBY KNIGHT'S SWEATER

It's entirely possible that the Indiana coach liked crimson tops because they matched the color of his face when he was angry.

BEAR BRYANT'S HAT

Jets owner Sonny Werblin gave the Bama icon his first houndstooth hat in 1964.

BJORN BORG'S HEADBAND

Flowing locks and a striped sweatband completed the Swede's aura of cool dominance.

STEVE SPURRIER'S VISOR

The Head Ball Coach has shaded his view at Florida and South Carolina.

THE CREAM of the crop at number 90 includes one defensive lineman whose playing days are done, and three still defining their careers on the field. So let's begin by looking at the bar set for others by **Neil Smith**. A defensive end who played mostly for the Chiefs from 1988 to 2000, Smith made it to six Pro Bowls and was voted onto one All-Pro team, in '93. That year he also led the league in sacks, with 15. For his career he took down the quarterback 104½ times.

That's a complete résumé. **Jason Pierre-Paul**, on the other hand, is just setting out. In 2011, his second season, he racked up 16½ sacks, was named All-Pro and won a Super Bowl with the Giants. But he's since been hurt and his numbers have suffered. **Ndamukong Suh** was another who got off to a quick start, making All-Pro as rookie in Detroit in 2010. But his freight train has made unscheduled stops in the towns of Dumb Penalty, Stompville and League Discipline. Perhaps Suh will harness his power and use it for good.

Which brings us to **Julius Peppers**, who also came into the league looking like a future great and has mostly fulfilled the promise. While not a true dominator, he has had eight seasons of double-digit sacks and has made eight Pro Bowls for the Panthers and the Bears. This choice here could easily change in 10 years, or less. But for now, sign us up for the Pep squad.

➤ THE VERDICT
JULIUS PEPPERS

CONTENDERS

NFL
Larry Brooks
Darnell Dockett
Jevon Kearse
Julius Peppers
Jason Pierre-Paul
Chuck Smith
Neil Smith
Ndamukong Suh

NHL
Joe Juneau

STAYING COOL IN THE 90S

While some players will hold their numbers hostage, demanding payment before it is surrendered, not everyone goes that way. When JULIUS PEPPERS signed with Chicago in 2010 and asked for 90, the Bears gave the number to him without even checking with second-year man JARRON GILBERT. When Peppers offered his new teammate remuneration anyway, Gilbert said, "It's all good."

CONTENDERS

NFL
Kevin Greene
Tamba Hali
Chester McGlockton
Robert Porcher
Justin Tuck
Cameron Wake

NHL
Sergei Fedorov
Steven Stamkos
John Tavares

AVOID UNWANTED ASSOCIATIONS

Who says that a number needs to be worn by a legend before it is retired? In Ottawa, 91 is unofficially on the shelf, but not because of a legacy of greatness. Quite the opposite. After 91 was worn by disappointing 1993 top overall pick ALEXANDRE DAIGLE, the Senators have since acquired two players (OLEG SAPRYKIN and KYLE TURRIS) who wore 91 for other teams. Neither opted to wear the number in Ottawa.

THE DEBATE

AT THE 1990 Goodwill Games in Seattle, **Sergei Fedorov** jumped from one team that wore red to another, defecting from the Soviet Union to play professionally in Detroit. But he was able to make himself at home, developing a relationship with tennis player and countrywoman Anna Kournikova and marrying her on the sly; few knew about the marriage until after it had ended in divorce. More happily he was a central figure in the so-called Red Army, the unit of five Russian players whom Detroit deployed to great success. Fedorov, swift on his skates, helped Detroit to three Stanley Cups, while being named league MVP in 1993–94 and twice being named the NHL's best defensive forward.

As the only player wearing 91 to achieve that kind of success, Fedorov is the clear choice, ahead of a crew of NFL players who reached All-Pro level but never, say, won a Defensive Player of the Year award or election to the Hall of Fame. **Kevin Greene**, the linebacker with the long blond hair, stands out as the best of the football choices. Greene twice led the NFL in sacks and brought down the quarterback 160 times in his career.

But the NFL currently boasts an intriguing collection of youthful pass rushing talent, including such 91s as **Tamba Hali**, **Chris Long**, **Cameron Wake**, **Ryan Kerrigan** and **Fletcher Cox**, among others. While it would be silly to make a prediction on the future of any of these players who (we fervently hope) have so much of their careers remaining, number 91's best days may be ahead.

➤ THE VERDICT
SERGEI FEDOROV

92

THE DEBATE

THE CONTEST for the leader at number 92 is no contest at all. Simply put, it has to be **Reggie White**. A strong candidate for greatest defensive end ever, White, possessed of enormous power and freakish agility, was a two-time Defensive Player of the Year. He sacked the quarterback 198 times. And that's not including the two years at the beginning of his career when the Minister of Defense had 23½ sacks for the Memphis Showboats of the USFL. So, Reggie White it is.

But the race for runner-up is a good one, involving four-time All-Pro defensive end and cheery morning-show host **Michael Strahan** and a player with a disposition notably less suited to lighthearted banter with Kelly Ripa, **James Harrison**. Strahan's résumé features 141½ sacks, including a record-setting 22½ in 2001, the season he won Defensive Player of the Year. (The dubious sack he touched down Brett Favre on a meaningless play irks, but 21½ legitimate sacks is still tremendous). Oh, and he's a 2014 Pro Football Hall of Fame inductee to boot.

While Strahan is known for his gap-toothed smile, Harrison arrived with a scowl that has remained. It took Harrison five years to stick on a roster and graduate from special teams, but once he became a starter at linebacker he played as if he had something to prove, becoming known as one of the league's most vicious hitters. In 2008 he had 16 sacks and was Defensive Player of the Year. The voting took place before the Super Bowl, in which his interception and 100-yard return for a touchdown was as great a play as you'll see. The fight he showed getting over the goal line, and throughout his career, is what lands Harrison in second place.

➤ THE VERDICT
REGGIE WHITE

196

IT CERTAINLY WORKED FOR HIM

The only NBA player to wear 92, DESHAWN STEVENSON assumed that number when he was traded to the Mavericks in 2010. In his somewhat disappointing career he had worn 2 and 9 at his previous stops, but by putting the two together he started some fire. Stevenson emerged as a defensive stopper in Dallas, especially against LeBron James in the NBA Finals as the Mavericks topped the Heat.

CONTENDERS

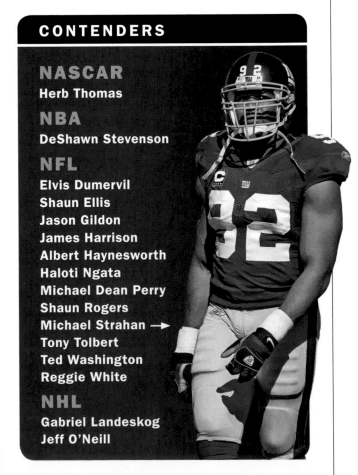

NASCAR
Herb Thomas

NBA
DeShawn Stevenson

NFL
Elvis Dumervil
Shaun Ellis
Jason Gildon
James Harrison
Albert Haynesworth
Haloti Ngata
Michael Dean Perry
Shaun Rogers
Michael Strahan ➤
Tony Tolbert
Ted Washington
Reggie White

NHL
Gabriel Landeskog
Jeff O'Neill

93

THE DEBATE

IT TAKES SOME chutzpah to declare that an active player is better than one already enshrined in the Hall of Fame. This is especially true when both men played the same position, and the Hall of Famer in question is not a relic who was by all accounts a terror on the Dayton Triangles in 1924, but an athlete current enough to have played his entire career in the age of SportsCenter.

It made sense to give camera time to **John Randle**, and not just because his attention-getting trademark mask of eyeblack would be the envy of raccoons and the Ultimate Warrior of WWE. With 137½ career sacks, including a league-leading 15½ in 1997 with the Vikings, the telegenic defensive lineman brought about the ruin of many an offensive game plan with his up-the-gut pressure.

On paper Randle seems to outpoint **Dwight Freeney**. They are both seven-time Pro Bowlers, but Randle currently leads Freeney in All-Pro teams, seven to three. Freeney has 108 career sacks (his best season: a league-leading 16 in 2004); with his '13 season ended by a torn quadriceps, it's hard to project that number will go up much, if at all. Now 34, Freeney has relied on speed as much as power, and the 30s tend not to be kind to speed rushers. He also suffered the plague of the modern front-seven player, being asked to switch position when the team shifts from the 4–3 to the 3–4. But when Freeney was young, he was something else. In his rookie season he forced nine fumbles. Another year he induced six, and another year, five. Randle never forced more than four in a season. Those forced fumbles speak to sudden disruptions. Freeney at his best was more of a terror than Randle, face paint or no.

➡ THE VERDICT
DWIGHT FREENEY

IT TAKES SOME SQUINTING

He has switched his number seven times in his career (six more the number of times he has changed his name). When he was in Sacramento from 2006 to '08, **METTA WORLD PEACE** wore 93. He chose the digits because he thought they looked like the letters QB, which is short for Queensbridge, the name of the public housing development in which (as Ron Artest) he grew up in New York City.

CONTENDERS

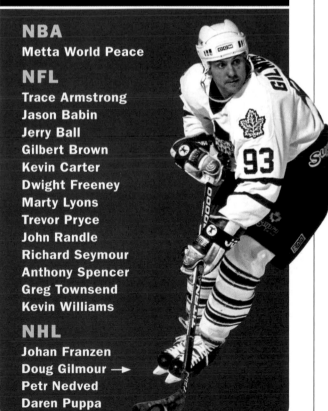

NBA
Metta World Peace

NFL
Trace Armstrong
Jason Babin
Jerry Ball
Gilbert Brown
Kevin Carter
Dwight Freeney
Marty Lyons
Trevor Pryce
John Randle
Richard Seymour
Anthony Spencer
Greg Townsend
Kevin Williams

NHL
Johan Franzen
Doug Gilmour ➡
Petr Nedved
Daren Puppa

94

THE DEBATE

HE WAS NO gentleman. **Charles Haley** was known for berating and bullying reporters, and for being crude and hostile toward his teammates. The time he urinated on 49ers teammate Tim Harris's car is one example that can be printed here. (For examples that can't be printed here, see Jeff Pearlman's excellent book *Boys Will Be Boys*.) These incidents, which no doubt lodge in the memory of those he offended, are often brought up by Haley's advocates as an explanation for why he is not in the Hall of Fame, despite being a finalist each year from 2010 to '14. On merit, his case is strong. While the edge rusher's sack totals are not overwhelming, with 100½ for his career, the one area in which he is unequaled is Super Bowl rings. He has five, and he is the only player who can say that. Haley wasn't just along for the ride. He was usually the best pass rusher on his title teams in Dallas and San Francisco; he was an essential ingredient to victory.

It's the winning that separates Haley from another Cowboy great, **DeMarcus Ware**. At age 31, the four-time All-Pro linebacker has already surpassed Haley's sack totals, and he's on the short list of the premier pass rushers of his day. But his Dallas teams were noted mainly for failed expectations. While it's certainly not fair to hang the Cowboys' shortcomings on their best defensive player—after all, Dick Butkus's Bears never won a title—this blank spot on Ware's résumé does stand out when you judge him side by side against Haley. One player can hold up a fist with a Super Bowl ring on each finger (and one for the thumb), and the other has no bling. Ware, now in Denver, might trade a couple of dozen sacks for the right to have one ring of his own.

 **THE VERDICT**

CHARLES HALEY

IT'S ALWAYS A HOME UNIFORM

It's a long way from Denver to Val-de-Marne, France, so Nuggets swingman **EVAN FOURNIER** wears 94 for the number of the *département* (a French level of government) to which Val-de-Marne corresponds. . . . **RYAN SMYTH** couldn't wear number 94 in the 2007 NHL All-Star Game because **YANIC PERREAULT**, another 94, was also voted in and had seniority. Smyth took 93.

CONTENDERS

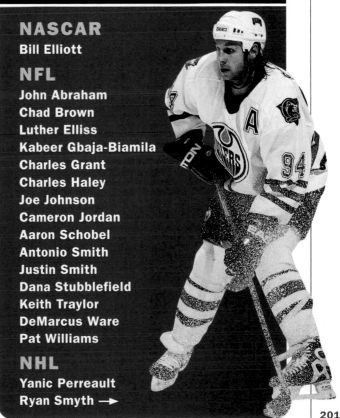

NASCAR
Bill Elliott

NFL
John Abraham
Chad Brown
Luther Elliss
Kabeer Gbaja-Biamila
Charles Grant
Charles Haley
Joe Johnson
Cameron Jordan
Aaron Schobel
Antonio Smith
Justin Smith
Dana Stubblefield
Keith Traylor
DeMarcus Ware
Pat Williams

NHL
Yanic Perreault
Ryan Smyth →

TAKING A NUMBER in the 90s did not come into vogue in the NFL until the last few decades, and in the NHL it was later than that. So the depth in these parts is thinner than a supermodel coming off a juice cleanse. But there are two guys here you would go into gridiron battle with anytime: **Greg Lloyd** and **Richard Dent**.

Lloyd was beloved in Pittsburgh for embodying the intensity that Steelers fans expect from their linebackers. His play upheld the legacy of Jack Lambert and Jack Ham, and Lloyd's best years—from 1991 through '95, when he made the Pro Bowl every season—coincided with a return of Pittsburgh to contention after a down period. On his watch the Steel Curtain seemed to rise again, even if not all the way to Super Bowl heights.

Dent, though, attained the summit. The 6' 5" defensive end, an unheralded eighth-round pick from Tennessee State in 1983, dominated opponents from the time he became a starter in his second season. That year he had 17½ sacks, and he followed up with a league-high 17 sacks as the Bears went 15–1. In the Super Bowl against the overmatched Patriots he forced two fumbles and had 1½ sacks, which earned him Super Bowl MVP. For a career that continued through '97, he had 137½ sacks and was named to four Pro Bowls. In 2011 Dent was elected to the Hall of Fame. Not bad for a late pick, and certainly enough to claim this number.

► THE VERDICT
RICHARD DENT

CONTENDERS

NFL

Sam Adams
Richard Dent
Greg Lloyd
Charles Johnson
Bryce Paup
Shaun Phillips
Kyle Williams
Kamerion Wimbley

NHL

Aleksey Morozov

LLOYD'S LONG SHADOW

In his first preseason Steelers linebacker JOEY PORTER wore the number 95, which had belonged to GREG LLOYD. But after a strong training camp in which he drew comparisons to his immediate predecessor, Porter decided to switch to 55 before the 1999 regular season, to create his own identity. In 2013 Pittsburgh first-round pick JARVIS JONES, unfazed by any comparison to Lloyd, requested and got 95.

COACH SAYS TO STAY LOW

His first choice was to wear 96. PAVEL BURE requested the number when he joined Vancouver in 1991 because he wanted to commemorate the day he arrived in North America, 9/6/91. But coach Pat Quinn didn't approve of players wearing high numbers, so Bure wore 10. Only after the Canucks acquired another high-numbered player, Alexander Mogilny (89), was Bure allowed to don 96. He switched back to 10 after two down years.

THE DEBATE

UNLESS SEATTLE is playing in the Super Bowl, it can be hard for a Seahawks player to gain national attention. That's especially true when the team stinks, and in 1992 the Seahawks were positively fetid, going 2–14. Yet amid all that remote losing that season, **Cortez Kennedy** was named Defensive Player of the Year, which tells you all you need know about how the defensive tackle could dominate the middle.

One of Kennedy's great weapons was his physique, which, as the above photo shows, would not have made him a candidate for the cover of *Men's Health*. "I like being big because it gives me confidence," Kennedy told SI in 1992. "Nobody wants to mess with me, and it helps me play my position. If I were small, I'd be a pretty boy. I'd have muscles, and I'd be standing in front of the mirror all the time. I don't want to be thin. I don't want to

be pretty. I just want to be the Tez." You certainly can't argue with Tez's results.

Kennedy's girth helps him loom large in another thin crowd. In second place, a considerable step down, is **Clyde Simmons**, who led the NFL in sacks with 19 for the Eagles in 1992, and might have wondered why Kennedy (and not he) was Defensive Player of the Year. Simmons wasn't one to raise a ruckus. Considering his production—he had 121½ career sacks—the defensive end cut a relatively subdued figure on a team with high-profile stars such as Randall Cunningham and Reggie White. But it's in a crowd of 96s that a low-key type such as Simmons can stand out.

➤ **THE VERDICT**
CORTEZ KENNEDY

97

IT'S THE RARE player in this book who has been named tops at a number while wearing it only part-time through his career. But the race here comes down to two 97s who have spent significant time with other numbers. **Jeremy Roenick** wore 27 for his first eight seasons in Chicago before graduating to the higher number in Phoenix, Philadelphia and Los Angeles. Then there's **Kurt Busch,** who drove the 97 car from 2000 to '05, but then moved along to race the number 2 car and, after that, cars 22, 51 and 78.

Busch's greatest season, though, did come as a 97. That was 2004, when he won the inaugural Chase for the Cup in thrilling fashion. In the last event of the season, at Homestead-Miami Speedway, he lost a tire coming into the pit but still managed to fight his way into a fifth-place finish, which was good enough for him to edge Jimmie Johnson in the overall standings by the narrowest of margins.

Roenick never had a season in which he soared as high as Busch did. But the nine-time All-Star (five of those honors came when he wore 97) enjoyed a long run as one of the more entertaining players in his sport and also one of the top Americans in his game. (He was just the third from the U.S. to score 500 goals.) And he wore 97 for longer than did Busch. In this race, that gets you points.

THE VERDICT
JEREMY ROENICK

CONTENDERS

NASCAR
Kurt Busch

NFL
Geno Atkins
Cornelius Bennett
La'Roi Glover
Patrick Kerney
Simeon Rice
Bryant Young

NHL
Jeremy Roenick

REMEMBERING A BROTHER

Panthers defenseman MATT GILROY wears 97 as a remembrance of his brother Timmy, who died from a head injury sustained in a bicycle accident when Matt was 9 and Timmy just shy of 8. Timmy wore 97 in youth hockey, and the night of his death, Matt told his mother he would always wear his brother's number. At Boston University the program didn't allow numbers higher than 35, but an exception was made for Gilroy.

98

THE TRUE MEANING OF CHANGE

For most of his career JASON COLLINS wore numbers 34 or 35, but in 2013 with the Celtics, he started wearing 98, a quiet move whose significance was revealed when Collins came out as gay after the season. The number was a tribute to Matthew Shepard, the gay Wyoming student who was tortured and murdered in 1998. In February 2014 Collins signed with the Nets, becoming the first openly gay male athlete active in a major U.S. sport.

THE DEBATE

IF YOU'RE CASTING a leading man, this is a tough spot, as there are many excellent players here, but not much star power. The biggest name is **Tony Siragusa**, but that has more to do with personality than with production. Even if you enjoy the Goose's sideline commentary or dug his antics on *Hard Knocks* back when he was with the Ravens, it's tough to hand this award to the zero-time Pro Bowler, not with more decorated players available.

It's tempting to choose **Brian Orakpo,** who hit the league in 2009 looking like the next great force-of-nature linebacker and made the Pro Bowl each of his first two seasons. While it's quite possible this athlete with the ever-popular "massive upside" will have many dominant seasons, he's also already had injuries to his shoulder, pectoral muscle and more. With so many careers derailed by injury, it makes sense to look for a player who has already done what he is going to do.

The best of that lot is **Casey Hampton.** The Steelers nosetackle was the heart of a consistently stout run defense from the time he arrived in Pittsburgh in 2001. The team was in the top three in the NFL in the category for 10 of the 12 seasons he played there, and he also was part of the group that brought Pittsburgh two Super Bowl titles. In Super Bowl XLIII, the Cardinals ran for a mere 33 yards. Not all of the credit for that goes to Hampton, but the effort began with him, and amid the collection of 98s, none have known more success on the field.

➤ THE VERDICT
CASEY HAMPTON

99

THE DEBATE

HE WANTED to wear 9 for the Sault Ste. Marie Greyhounds, out of admiration for Gordie Howe. But that number was taken, so **Wayne Gretzky** chose a uniform with two 9s and wound up breaking the career records owned by Howe and scoring more points and goals than everyone else who ever put on skates. Among Gretzky's superlatives: He exceeded 200 points in a season four times, whereas no other player has done it once. He holds the record for goals in a season, with 92, and he was such a masterly passer that he would be the NHL's alltime leading scorer on assists alone. He won four Stanley Cups, all in Edmonton, and perhaps more impressive, he made fans in Los Angeles care about hockey when he was traded to the Kings in 1988. After he played his final NHL game—fittingly, in '99—for the Rangers, he took to the Madison Square Garden ice and even though his greatest moments had been elsewhere, the ovation went on for a good quarter hour, just because the New York fans knew they were in the presence of the best ever. The league declared that after Gretzky no NHL player would wear 99 again.

The race for second has strong contenders, including **Warren Sapp** and the best active defensive end in football, **J.J. Watt**, but the choice is **George Mikan**. He reeled off three straight scoring titles from 1949 to '51. Even though the NBA then consisted of relatively few teams, "Mr. Basketball" is important because he was the game's first great big man. Before he came along the game belonged to guards, but the way Mikan dominated, everyone wanted a big guy in the middle. When Mikan died in 2005, Shaquille O'Neal paid his funeral expenses. "Without 99," said O'Neal, "there is no me."

➤ THE VERDICT

WAYNE GRETZKY

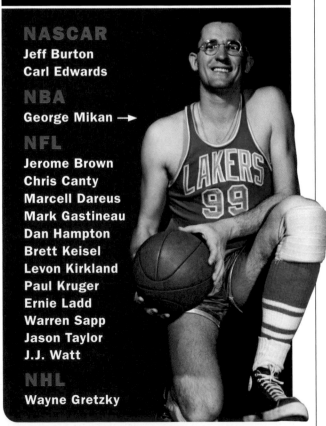

WHERE THE WILD THINGS ARE

Perhaps because it is an extreme, number 99 has attracted some, er, *diverse* personalities, including reliever MITCH WILLIAMS, who switched to it in 1993. It was suggested that Williams chose the number in imitation of pitcher Ricky (Wild Thing) Vaughn from the movie *Major League*, but Williams said the choice was a tribute to another free spirit: the long-haired, sack-dancing, MARK GASTINEAU.

CONTENDERS

NASCAR
Jeff Burton
Carl Edwards

NBA
George Mikan

NFL
Jerome Brown
Chris Canty
Marcell Dareus
Mark Gastineau
Dan Hampton
Brett Keisel
Levon Kirkland
Paul Kruger
Ernie Ladd
Warren Sapp
Jason Taylor
J.J. Watt

NHL
Wayne Gretzky

Cover (*left to right, from top*): Chuck Solomon, Walter Iooss Jr., Paul Kennedy, Richard Mackson, Walter Iooss Jr., George Tiedemann/GT Images, John W. McDonough, Heinz Kluetmeier, MLB Photos/Getty Images, Neil Leifer, George Tiedemann/GT Images, John Biever (2), Walter Iooss Jr. (2), John G. Zimmerman; **Back Cover** (*left to right, from top*): John Biever, James Drake, John G. Zimmerman (2), Peter Read Miller, Neil Leifer, Walter Iooss Jr., Andy Hayt; **Page 3:** Neil Leifer; **Pages 4-5:** David E. Klutho; **Page 6:** Tim Smith/Getty Images; **Pages 9-10:** Porter Binks; **Page 11:** John Biever; **Pages 14-15** (*clockwise from top left*): Walter Iooss Jr, John W. McDonough, Neil Leifer; **Pages 16-17** (*clockwise from top left*): Ben Van Hook, Ronald C. Modra, Simon Bruty; **Pages 18-19** (*clockwise from left*): Chuck Solomon, Robert Beck, Heinz Kluetmeier; **Pages 20-21** (*from left*): Al Tielemans, Bettmann/Corbis, George Tiedemann/GT Images; **Pages 22-23** (*clockwise from top left*): Tom DiPace, James Drake, John Biever; **Pages 24-25** (*from left*): Bettmann/Corbis, Heinz Kluetmeier, Robert Beck; **Pages 26-27** (*clockwise from top left*): Andrew D. Bernstein/Getty Images, Robert Huntzinger, John W. McDonough; **Pages 28-29** (*from left*): Tony Triolo, Peter Read Miller, John G. Zimmerman; **Pages 30-31** (*clockwise from left*): Bettmann/Corbis, Arthur Daley/Diamond Images/Getty Images, Richard Mackson; **Pages 32-33** (*from left*): Robert Beck, Hy Peskin, James Drake; **Page 35:** John Iacono; **Pages 36-37** (*clockwise from left*): George Tiedemann/GT Images, Walter Iooss Jr., Tom DiPace; **Pages 38-39** (*clockwise from left*): John W. McDonough, Lou Capozzola, John Biever; **Pages 40-41** (*clockwise from left*): John W. McDonough, Doug Pensinger/Getty Images, John W. McDonough; **Pages 42-43** (*from left*): John W. McDonough, Walter Iooss Jr., John Biever; **Pages 44-45** (*clockwise from top left*): Hy Peskin, Long Photography, Inc., Andy Hayt; **Pages 46-47** (*clockwise from left*): Walter Iooss Jr., John Iacono, Lou Capozzola; **Pages 48-49** (*from left*): John W. McDonough, Richard Mackson, Walter Iooss Jr.; **Pages 50-51** (*clockwise from left*): John W. McDonough, Walter Iooss Jr. (2); **Pages 52-53** (*from left*): Robert Beck, Peter Read Miller, George Tiedemann/GT Images; **Pages 54-55** (*clockwise from left*): Walter Iooss Jr., Chuck Solomon, John W. McDonough; **Page 57:** Manny Millan; **Pages 58-59** (*from left*): Walter Iooss Jr., John Biever, Jacqueline Duvoisin; **Pages 60-61** (*from left*): John W. McDonough, Robert Beck, John Biever; **Pages 62-63** (*clockwise from top left*): John Iacono, Al Tielemans, John W. McDonough; **Pages 64-65** (*from left*): John Biever, Lou Capozzola, David Durochik/MLB Photos/Getty Images; **Pages 66-67** (*clockwise from top left*): John W. McDonough, Frank Hurley/New York Daily News Archive/Getty Images, Richard Mackson; **Pages 68-69** (*from left*): Walter Iooss Jr., Brad Mangin, V.J. Lovero; **Pages 70-71** (*from left*): Damian Strohmeyer, Heinz Kluetmeier, Peter Read Miller; **Pages 72-73** (*from left*): Bob Rosato, Fred Kaplan, Walter Iooss Jr.; **Pages 74-75** (*clockwise from left*): Peter Read Miller, David Walberg, John Biever; **Pages 76-77** (*clockwise from left*): Peter Read Miller, Heinz Kluetmeier, Herb Scharfman; **Page 79:** Al Tielemans; **Pages 80-81** (*clockwise from left*): David E. Klutho, John W. McDonough, Peter Read Miller; **Pages 82-83** (*clockwise from top left*): Walter Iooss Jr., Richard Mackson, John W. McDonough; **Pages 84-85** (*clockwise from top left*): Neil Leifer, Andy Hayt, Focus on Sport/Getty Images; **Pages 86-87** (*from left*): NFL Photos/AP, Richard Mackson, AP; **Pages 88-89** (*clockwise from left*): John Biever, Simon Bruty, Brad Mangin; **Pages 90-91** (*from left*): Brad Mangin (2), Greg Nelson; **Pages 92-93** (*clockwise from top left*): Michael Ivins/Boston Red Sox/Getty Images, Walter Iooss Jr., Al Tielemans; **Pages 94-95** (*from left*): Hy Peskin, Carlos M. Saavedra, Damian Strohmeyer; **Pages 96-97** (*clockwise from top left*): Brad Mangin, Damian Strohmeyer, Ian Tomlinson/Getty Images; **Pages 98-99** (*from left*): Walter Iooss Jr., John G. Zimmerman, David E. Klutho; **Page 101:** David E. Klutho; **Pages 102-103** (*clockwise from left*): NFL Photos/AP, Gene Lower/Slingshot, Nathaniel S. Butler/NBAE/Getty Images; **Pages 104-105** (*from left*): Bob Rosato, John D. Hanlon, Richard Meek; **Pages 106-107** (*clockwise from top left*): Chuck Solomon, Mark Kauffman, John W. McDonough; **Pages 108-109** (*clockwise from left*): Eric Schweikardt, Nathaniel S. Butler/NBAE/Getty Images, Damian Strohmeyer; **Pages 110-111** (*clockwise from left*): Syracuse University/Collegiate Images/Getty Images, Fred Kaplan, Walter Iooss Jr.; **Pages 112-113** (*from left*): Focus on Sport/Getty Images, Walter Iooss Jr.; **Pages 114-115** (*from left*): John Iacono, Bruce Dierdorff/Getty Images, Mickey Pfleger; **Pages 116-117** (*from left*): Scott Hallernan/Getty Images, Walter Iooss Jr., Chuck Solomon; **Pages 118-119** (*clockwise from left*): Courtesy of Gerald R. Ford Library, Nigel Kinrade/NKP, John Biever; **Pages 120-121** (*from left*): Neil Leifer, John W. McDonough, Neil Leifer; **Pages 122-123** (*clockwise from top left*): Neil Leifer, James Drake, Marvin E. Newman, John Biever, Marvin E. Newman, Rich Clarkson, James Drake, David Liam Kyle, V.J. Lovero, Joe Robbins, Carl Skalak; **Pages 124-125** (*from left*): Bill Frakes, Walter Iooss Jr., John W. McDonough; **Pages 126-127** (*clockwise from top left*): John Biever, Neil Leifer, Robert Beck; **Pages 128-129** (*from left*): John Biever, Patrick McDermott/Getty Images, Tony Tomsic; **Pages 130-131** (*clockwise from top left*):

Buena Vista Pictures/Photofest, Neil Leifer, Jerry Wachter; **Pages 132-133** (*clockwise from left*): Fred Kaplan, Phil Huber, John Biever; **Pages 134-135** (*from left*): Bill Baptist/NBAE/Getty Images, V.J. Lovero, John W. McDonough; **Pages 136-137** (*clockwise from left*): John Iacono, Ann Heisenfelt/AP, John W. McDonough; **Pages 138-139** (*from left*): Greg Trott/AP, Chuck Solomon, Manny Rubio/USA TODAY Sports; **Pages 140-141** (*from left*): Walter Iooss Jr., Jim Campbell/Getty Images; **Pages 142-143** (*clockwise from top left*): Heinz Kluetmeier, Andy Hayt, AP, Hy Peskin, Rich Clarkson, Heinz Kluetmeier, Walter Iooss Jr., AP, Greg Nelson, Jamie Squire/Getty Images, Focus on Sport/Getty Images, Stuart Smith; **Pages 144-145** (*clockwise from top left*): Damian Strohmeyer, Bettmann/Corbis, John G. Zimmerman; **Pages 146-147** (*from left*): Darryl Norenberg/USA TODAY Sports, Neil Leifer; **Pages 148-149** (*clockwise from top left*): Damian Strohmeyer, Walter Iooss Jr., Lou Capozzola; **Pages 150-151** (*from left*): Damian Strohmeyer, NFL Photos/AP; **Pages 152-153** (*from left*): Al Tielemans, David E. Klutho, Neil Leifer; **Pages 154-155** (*clockwise from left*): Anthony Neste, David E. Klutho, Peter Brouillet/Getty Images; **Pages 156-157** (*from left*): Lou Capozzola, Al Tielemans; **Pages 158-159** (*clockwise from top left*): Neil Leifer, Robert Beck, Tony Triolo, Tom DiPace, Bettmann/Corbis, Cliff Welch/Icon SMI, Charles Rex Arbogast/AP, Barry Gossage/NBAE/Getty Images, Tony Dejak/AP (2), Manny Millan, Peter Read Miller, V.J. Lovero, Darryl Norenberg/USA TODAY Sports; **Pages 160-161** (*from left*): Neil Leifer, Marvin E. Newman; **Pages 162-163** (*clockwise from top left*): Michael Perez/AP, Neil Leifer, Ronald C. Modra/Sports Imagery/Getty Images; **Pages 164-165** (*clockwise from left*): Manny Millan, Osamu Honda/AP, Robert B. Stanton/Getty Images; **Pages 166-167** (*clockwise from top left*): Robert Beck, Walter Iooss Jr., NFL Photos/AP; **Pages 168-169** (*clockwise from left*): Walter Iooss Jr., Brad Mangin, NFL Photos/AP; **Pages 170-171** (*from left*): AP, Library of Congress; **Pages 172-173** (*from left*): Peter Brouillet/Getty Images, Neil Leifer; **Pages 174-175** (*clockwise from top left*): Stephen Wade/Getty Images, Chuck Solomon, Scott Cunningham, Rich Pilling/MLB Photos/Getty Images, Glenn James, Tom DiPace, Harry How/Getty Images, John Biever, Steve Lipofsky/BasketballPhoto.com, Gary Bogdon, AP, John Iacono; **Pages 176-177** (*clockwise from top left*): Brad Mangin, Thomas E. Witte, David E. Klutho; **Pages 178-179** (*from left*): David E. Klutho, James Drake, Mike Thomas/AP; **Pages 180-181:** Walter Iooss Jr. (2); **Pages 182-183** (*clockwise from top left*): John Biever, Damian Strohmeyer, V.J. Lovero; **Pages 184-185** (*clockwise from left*): Neil Leifer, Heinz Kluetmeier, Bob Rosato; **Pages 186-187** (*from left*): John Biever, Lou Capozzola; **Pages 188-189** (*clockwise from left*): Neil Leifer, Paul Connors/AP, Peter Read Miller; **Pages 190-191** (*clockwise from top left*): Richard C. Lewis, Tony Tomsic/Getty Images, Simon Bruty; **Pages 192-193** (*clockwise from top left*): Fred Vuich, John W. McDonough, Walter Iooss Jr. (2), Bob Rosato, John W. McDonough, John Iacono; **Pages 194-195** (*from left*): Darren Carroll, Scott Rovak/UPI/Landov; **Pages 196-197** (*clockwise from top left*): John W. McDonough, Tom DiPace, Bob Rosato; **Pages 198-199** (*clockwise from left*): Bob Rosato, Greg Nelson, Jim Leary; **Pages 200-201** (*clockwise from left*): Brad Mangin, Garrett W. Ellwood/NBAE/Getty Images, David E. Klutho; **Pages 202-203** (*from left*): John W. McDonough, Stephen Dunn/Getty Images; **Pages 204-205** (*from left*): Lou Capozzola, Bill Frakes; **Pages 206-207** (*clockwise from top left*): Focus on Sport/Getty Images, Paul J. Bereswill/Hockey Hall of Fame, Bettmann/Corbis; **Page 208:** Courtesy of National Baseball Hall of Fame and Museum

Only worn once: Eddie Gaedel sported this ⅛ jersey as a pinch hitter for the St. Louis Browns in 1951.

TIME HOME ENTERTAINMENT **Publisher** Jim Childs **Vice President, Brand & Digital Strategy** Steven Sandonato **Executive Director, Marketing Services** Carol Pittard **Executive Director, Retail & Special Sales** Tom Mifsud **Executive Publishing Director** Joy Butts **Director, Bookazine Development & Marketing** Laura Adam **Vice President, Finance** Vandana Patel **Publishing Director** Megan Pearlman **Assistant Director, Special Sales** Ilene Schreider **Senior Book Production Manager** Susan Chodakiewicz **Brand Manager** Michele Bové **Associate Prepress Manager** Alex Voznesenskiy **Editorial Director** Stephen Koepp

Special thanks to Dick Friedman, Geoff Michaud, Dan Larkin, Gerry Burke, Hai Tan, Sandra Vallejos, Emily Kaplan, Mike Bebernes, Jose Montiel and Nicholas Friar for their very valued assistance on this project.